D1409208

Confessions
of a
MOLLY MORMON

Love & joy!

Elona

Shelley

Confessions *of a* MOLLY MORMON

Trading Perfectionism for Peace,
Fear for Faith, Judging for Joy

ELONA K. SHELLEY

SΔP
Summit View Publishing
Orem, Utah

Lyrics to *A Child's Prayer* by Janice Kapp Perry © Janice Kapp Perry. Used by permission of the author.

Cover image *Woman cheering in field* (#20530331) by luna4 © Royalty-Free/iStockphoto
Cover design and page layout by Jennie Williams

Summit View Publishing
Orem, Utah 84097
www.SummitViewPublishing.com or www.sviewp.com

ISBN-13: 978-0-9818692-7-8
ISBN-10: 0-9818692-7-0

Printed in the United States of America
10 9 8 7 6 5 4 3 2 1

This book is printed on acid free paper.

To my beloved
husband,
children,
and grandchildren.

And to all those seeking abundant
truth,
peace,
faith,
and joy.

CONTENTS

Acknowledgments. ix

Introduction: Falling Off the Molly Mormon Pedestal
The truth and nothing but the truth. 1

My Seven Confessions

1. God and His Tattletale Angels
Learning to understand and love Heavenly Father. 9
    I confess that I felt no love for God.
    Today I rejoice in my deep love for God, and for His
        amazing love for each of His children.

2. The Iron Rod as a Weapon of Self-Destruction
Using the scriptures to help me keep my change of heart 23
    I confess that I resented the scriptures.
    Today I rejoice and *rejoice* in the gift of the scriptures!

3. Cold Floors and Aching Knees
Making prayer a pleasure 39
    I confess that my prayers were mostly a matter of routine.
    Today I rejoice in the strength and peace prayer brings to
        my life.

4. You Can Watch *Johnny Lingo* Only So Many Times
Allowing the Sabbath to fulfill its divine purpose. 53
    I confess that I dreaded Sundays.
    Today I rejoice in the gift of the Sabbath day.

5. Let the Hunger Pains Begin

Finding joy in observing the fast God has chosen 69
    I confess that fasting mostly meant just going hungry.
    Today I rejoice in fasting as a pathway to freedom and
        oneness with God.

6. Even My Hosanna Shout Wasn't Good Enough

Discovering the treasures of temple worship 83
    I confess that I found the temple confusing and boring.
    Today I rejoice in the sweet influence the temple brings to
        my life.

7. Neighbors—Who Needs Them?

Joyfully sharing God's love 97
    I confess that the commandment to love your neighbor
        seemed impossible.
    Today I gratefully rejoice in the love that constantly pours
        into my life.

Conclusion: I Glory in My Jesus!

From wretched to rejoicing 115

Appendix 125

Notes 171

ACKNOWLEDGMENTS

While working on this book over the past few years, I have been privileged to receive assistance from several very* capable editors. Without them this book would surely be much less readable. Their patience has been remarkable. Their encouragement has lifted me in times of doubt, and has helped me continue the task, even though I've taken many detours along the way.

I'm deeply indebted to a multitude of writers whose words have spoken to my heart and left their imprint on my soul. I'm likewise grateful to all who have personally engaged with me in conversations of the heart. You've enriched my life and increased my joy. Thank you.

I've chosen to use endnotes for all references, hoping to make the book as conversational as possible. This format is as close as I can come to sitting down with the reader and sharing the feelings of my heart. I've also chosen not to strictly follow all of the rules of punctuation and grammar that my editors so

---

* One of these wonderful editors told me I shouldn't use the word "very" very often, if at all, because it adds ~~very~~ little. She also suggested that I should use italics and exclamation points *very* sparingly! Consequently you will find fewer italics and exclamation points than I had in earlier drafts, but you'll still find more than she recommended. My daughter says that if this editor knew me personally, she would better understand all my exclamation points and my excessive use of adjectives. I realize I do get carried away sometimes, but I feel things ~~very~~ deeply, and I'm ~~very~~ eager to communicate exactly what I'm feeling!

aptly pointed out to me. In a few cases, following the rules felt awkward and disruptive to me. I take full responsibility for any errors. Although my editors deserve the highest praise, I haven't mentioned their names because I don't want them to be embarrassed when they notice things that don't match their standards. They know who they are, and I sincerely thank each one of them.

I will, however, name my husband, Monte, and my daughter, Christina Shelley Albrecht. I cannot thank them enough for the time and effort they have freely given me to bring about this book. They have stood by me through more than anyone should ever have to—reading, rereading, and suggesting possibilities that weren't always warmly welcomed. Without them this book would still be stuck in my computer. They— along with my mother and my son David—have provided me with the constant support my distractible nature required to complete this project. I truly appreciate, love, and adore them!

Many others have had a part in bringing this book into being. Friends and family have been encouraging and supportive. Some have shared wisdom from their professions. Others have reviewed and shared their thoughts about my writing. Still others have eased my responsibilities so I could spend more time on writing and revising. For me, it definitely takes a village! I sincerely appreciate each member of the village that has made this book possible.

Most of all, I want to acknowledge my indebtedness to God. He has been my underlying strength and joy throughout this lengthy endeavor. I'm constantly amazed and humbled by His goodness and His endless confidence in me.

INTRODUCTION

FALLING OFF THE
MOLLY MORMON PEDESTAL

The Truth and Nothing but the Truth

I absolutely love, worship, and adore our Savior Jesus Christ. Every single day, I rejoice in the beautiful truths of His gospel. I also rejoice in my relationship with a loving Heavenly Father and the knowledge that He desires me to live joyfully. Truly, my heart overflows with gratitude for the blessings I receive as an active member of The Church of Jesus Christ of Latter-day Saints. However, for many years, those were not my sentiments at all. In fact, in many ways, they were quite the opposite.

Even though I had a generally peaceful and safe childhood, during my earliest years, I developed a deeply fearful mindset. Most of my experiences, including the teachings I received about God and the principles of the Church, were processed through the distorting lens of fear. I felt certain that my true self was totally unacceptable, both to other people and to God. As time passed, my misguided perceptions dominated my thoughts, creating an ever-increasing sense of inadequacy in my heart and mind.

The struggle to reconcile my fearful beliefs with the doctrines of faith and hope set forth by the Church increased as I became an adult. Time and time again, I saw myself falling short of

God's many commandments, floundering in the endless stream of counsel that flowed from Church leaders. I was afraid that if other people were aware of my internal struggles, they'd think I wasn't a good Mormon, so I did my best to hide the truth and press on. I tried to compensate for my shortcomings by devoting excessive amounts of time and effort to Church service, but no matter how much I did, I never felt like I had done enough to measure up to God's stringent standards.

Eventually I was given experiences that taught me to see God and the Church through different eyes. My new perceptions were so freeing and joyful that I couldn't help sharing them with anyone who would listen. The more I shared, the more I discovered that I hadn't been alone. Many people, particularly mothers, identified with those same fears and frustrations.

I continued to gratefully share my newfound truths whenever an opportunity presented itself, but I had no desire to write a book. In fact, during the laborious task of revising an article I wrote for an LDS women's magazine,[1] I vowed I would never attempt a book. However, the Lord warns us that His ways are not our ways. Consequently, this book is a part of my humble response to the unrelenting insistence of the Spirit.

Before I plunge into the revealing waters of confession, I must admit that there was never a time when I considered myself good enough to be labeled a "Molly Mormon." It hadn't occurred to me that anyone else might identify me that way either—that is, until the day I went to have my hair cut by a beautician in my neighborhood whom I will call Janet. (Alternate names have been used throughout the book.)

Recent boundary changes had put our homes in the same ward, and I had been called to be the new Relief Society president. Since Janet wasn't very active, I hoped my need for her haircutting services would open a door of friendship, and perhaps help her feel more comfortable at church. My previous contact with her had been minimal, but a couple of people had warned me that she could be quite abrupt and outspoken, so I entered her salon that day feeling somewhat apprehensive.

However, hair appointments have a way of relaxing minds and loosening tongues. Within moments, we were engaged in an animated conversation that lasted well over an hour. Somewhere between the details of her frustrations with a rebellious teenage daughter and my struggles with a gay son, she suddenly paused to exclaim, "Hey, I think I might like you after all. I thought you were one of those perfect little Molly Mormons who knows nothing about real life, but I can see that I was wrong!"

I burst out laughing. Even before I realized someone had placed me on that precarious Molly Mormon pedestal, I had already fallen off.

Thankfully, I had abandoned my desire to be the perfect "Molly Mormon" much earlier, but for many stress filled years, Molly had been my obsession. And why wouldn't she be? She was everything I aspired to. She was organized, efficient, and always in control. Not only was she an attentive and charming wife, she was also the mother of several immaculately groomed, brilliantly creative, and perfectly behaved children.

Her home was spotless yet comfortable. She sewed all of her family's clothing and promptly took care of any mending that needed to be done. Each week she made delicious whole wheat bread, often dropping off a loaf to someone who needed a little extra love or encouragement. She canned hundreds of jars of homegrown fruits and vegetables each summer and generously shared the bounties of her flourishing garden. She served three delicious, carefully balanced meals every day, and of course she made full use of her ample food storage, which she rotated regularly.

Without fail, Molly got up early each morning, studying the scriptures for at least thirty minutes before going out for an invigorating five-mile run. She magnified her church callings, volunteered at her children's school, worked on family history, and attended the temple every week. She also babysat for her neighbors so they, too, could go to the temple. No matter how much she had to do, she was always calm and pleasant. I could go on listing the virtues of this amazing woman, but I'm sure you already get the picture. Suffice it to say, Molly was absolutely everything I thought I should be.

When people spoke disparagingly of my idol, I felt defensive. Wasn't Molly the perfect disciple of Christ? Didn't she do everything a good LDS woman was supposed to do, always without hesitation or complaint? Personally I envied all those Molly Mormons out there whose praises were sung in *Ensign* articles, sacrament meeting talks, and Relief Society lessons. Obviously they'd already secured their place in the celestial kingdom. When the trumpet sounded, they would walk confidently right through those guarded gates, sit down with their Peter Perfect husbands, and rejoice with their circle of celestial children.

I desperately tried to be like those inspiring Mollies so that I, too, could qualify for that coveted, ultimate blessing *someday.* But I had a huge problem: I couldn't seem to discipline myself enough to conquer even one of the many weaknesses plaguing my life *today.* Furthermore, in spite of my constant nagging— oops, I mean "loving persuasion"—I couldn't get my husband and children to do everything I thought *they* were supposed to be doing, either. Regardless of my frantic attempts to prepare our family for that marvelous, celestial eventuality, it appeared that none of us were celestial material.

Zealous efforts to increase my worthiness, by magnifying my callings and serving others, were rewarded with lavish praise and sincere appreciation. However, I struggled to appease an ever-mounting sense of guilt, because I often found more pleasure in serving *others* than in attending to the needs of my own family. In spite of my passionate resolve to find a balance, I was always lacking somewhere. Molly's coveted level of perfection remained completely out of my grasp. With such a chasm between my reality and my lofty ideals, it's no wonder I often found myself engaged in a losing battle with depression.

For many long and stress filled years, I was unaware of the chokehold the Molly illusion had on my life. I thought I was simply doing my very best to live the gospel. Once I was no longer a prisoner to Molly's deception, I became free to explore the origins of those elusive ideals and the reasons for my misguided drive for perfection.

Some of my earliest memories include being taught that strict obedience to all of God's commandments would bring me happiness, shield me from temptation, and get me into the celestial kingdom after I died so I could live with Jesus and Heavenly Father forever. This devotion to obedience seemed to be the central focus of the people I most trusted, so I firmly set my course to follow every commandment to the letter. The praise I received for knowing and doing what I was "supposed to do" felt wonderful. It really *did* make me feel happy, so keeping that praise rolling in became my urgent desire. I began trying to hide or to somehow compensate for anything that might jeopardize my happiness, my worthiness of praise.

After I became a teenager, one of my Young Women leaders taught a class on goal setting. She said we would be able to reach our goals more readily if we wrote them down and reviewed them daily. I eagerly jumped on the bandwagon, buying brightly colored notebooks, and making copious lists of all the wonderful things I would now be able to accomplish as I worked my way to perfection.

To my great dismay, I repeatedly found that I was still unable to make everything happen the way I wanted. Even when I *did* manage to reach a specific goal, such as reading The Book of Mormon from cover to cover or earning a perfect GPA, the resulting "happiness" was disappointingly short-lived. All too quickly it was swallowed up by a wave of discouragement as I contemplated the ever-increasing list of goals remaining before me.

As I moved on in life and became a mother, a similar pattern unfolded. My children brought me immeasurable joy, but being responsible for their spiritual growth multiplied my fears and frustrations. These precious little ones needed to be carefully prepared for the celestial kingdom, or we would never qualify as an eternal family.

The thought of being separated from my husband and children was unbearable, so I made endless lists of goals to avert that tragedy. Whether I wrote them on paper or carried them around in my head, the lists were always there to remind me that I was completely and utterly failing. While my Molly Mormon obsession continued to thrive, the crushing weight of perfectionism left my guilt-ridden spirit struggling for survival.

About five years before that hair appointment with Janet, my hopes for eventual happiness teetered precariously. Our oldest son, David, who had just turned sixteen, was spinning out of control, and I could see no way to make things end well. Little did I know that two dramatic events would soon transform my perception of happiness, along with my entire understanding of God.

The first event occurred on a warm spring day when David nervously approached me and informed me that he was gay. My fragile world shattered. All of my fleeting Molly Mormon hopes and dreams were annihilated in a single blow, and an overwhelming season of sorrow ensued. Despair shrouded my life throughout the months that followed, and for a time, I was barely able to function. All hope of happiness—present or future—had vanished.

The second event came in the midst of my darkest hour. Without warning, God wrapped me in the arms of His indescribable love and released me from the iron fist of my agonizing misconceptions. Gently, mercifully, He introduced me to the glorious light of this undeniable truth: God never intended me to be a Molly Mormon!

By divine design, I am a *Molly Mortal*, who like every other mortal, can joyfully look to a loving Savior for healing and peace. At last I understood. Life isn't about attaining perfection by completing a comprehensive checklist of noble goals. Life is about knowing and loving God.

Without realizing it, I had focused my quest for perfection on my own mortal power to accomplish, rather than on Christ's divine power to redeem. Though many things on my Molly Mormon lists were completely appropriate to do—even needful in many circumstances—I finally realized that real happiness comes from devotion to God, and true devotion to God can never come from a list. It can only come from the heart.

Confessions of a Molly Mormon exposes seven former attitudes that I once tried to hide, hoping to maintain the *appearance* of a righteous Latter-day Saint woman. Today I openly confess these attitudes, because in doing so, the way is paved for me to testify of the joyful, life-giving freedom the Savior offers.

Embracing the weakness of mortality has allowed me to accept life as a beautiful gift designed to help me experience God's guidance, His mercy, and His endless love. As long as the earth is my home, I know I will have challenges, but through Christ's amazing grace, this Molly Mortal has learned that it is possible to trade perfectionism for peace, fear for faith, and judging for joy.

1

GOD AND HIS TATTLETALE ANGELS

Learning to Understand and Love Heavenly Father

I confess that I felt no love for God.

Because I was born into an active LDS family, going to church was as natural for me as going to bed at night. It was just what we did. Each Sunday morning as ten o'clock approached, my parents could be found hastily herding their straggling flock of seven children into the old Chevy sedan. It took almost ten minutes to cover the three and a half miles of country road between our home and the church, and there was no way in the world we were going to make it on time.

Though the kitchen clock was always set ten minutes fast, that never solved the problem. We were usually leaving the house at about the time we should have been arriving at the chapel. The drive gave us time to argue about whose fault it was that we were late this week, and to be instructed on what we needed to do "next time" so it wouldn't happen again. Regardless of what was said or done, the scene almost always repeated itself the following week, with only slight variation.

Church was generally a friendly place, although there were those few stately old ladies who could be counted on to give disapproving scowls whenever someone violated their strict code of conduct. The majority of our priesthood leaders were farmers who began their chores long before dawn and labored in their fields until it was too dark to work anymore. A few even had tractors with headlights so they could extend their working hours.

In the hot summer months, they often got up in the middle of the night to attend to irrigation water, setting dams by the light of a flashlight, a lantern, or the radiant moon. Even in the winter, they seldom had a reprieve from the rigorous demands of their profession, so they treasured the rest provided by the Sabbath.

These men were passionate about their farming, and they were passionate about their religion. I can still see some of them standing before the congregation with fiery eyes, vigorously pounding the pulpit while loudly proclaiming the need to repent because God didn't let anyone into the celestial kingdom who wasn't perfect. Perhaps that is when I first began to think that I could never be good enough for God.

The idea that God was harsh and difficult to please was reinforced almost every time I went to church. We often sang a hymn that warned,

> Angels above us are silent notes taking
> Of ev'ry action; then do what is right![1]

Another hymn reminded us that

> holy angels
> Watch your actions night and day,
> And they keep a sacred record
> Of the good and bad you say.[2]

It seemed obvious that those watchful angels were heavenly tattletales who took their notes about my naughty behavior to God so He could determine the proper punishment for each bad thing I did. I thought He got really mad whenever I didn't "do what is right." When things didn't go well for me, I wondered which misbehavior I was being punished for and what greater punishment might be waiting to slam me later.

Many stories from the scriptures verified my misconceptions. It seemed like God was always getting angry at people for something. Even though I didn't throw rocks at prophets or bow down to idols, I clearly didn't follow all of the commandments I had been taught. To make matters worse, I kept discovering more and more new commandments all the time. I was undoubtedly in serious trouble with God.

When I heard about the big fire that would soon be coming to burn up all of the bad people and bring an end to the world, I was terrified. I envisioned my younger sister and me as the two people who the scriptures say will be standing in the field when the massive cleansing fire comes sweeping through.[3] In my mind, I could see my sister left untouched, but I was quickly burned to oblivion because of my sins. It was confusing to be told that Heavenly Father loved everyone, when He kept destroying people or pouring out painful punishments upon them.

Of course I liked hearing the tender stories of Jesus. Probably my favorite was the one where He raised the little girl from the dead, because I had a huge fear of dying and finding myself in a strange place without my family. I also loved to hear about the miracles Christ performed for people who were sick or blind. I was especially delighted by the story of Christ scolding His apostles for trying to send people away when they just wanted Him to bless their children.

However, these loving stories didn't seem to apply to me, because even though I *wanted* to be good, for some reason, I kept being *bad*. Jesus taught that we shouldn't tell lies, but sometimes I lied because I was sure my mom would spank me if I told the truth. Jesus wanted me to be unselfish, but I didn't like to share. Whenever we had treats, I always wanted the biggest cookie or the biggest piece of candy for myself.

I wasn't supposed to steal, but sometimes I sneaked a dime out of Mother's crystal bowl to go to the Valley Merc at lunchtime and buy a treat that I really, really wanted. Perhaps worst of all, I was secretly fascinated with the "forbidden" parts of my body. With all my sins, surely Jesus wouldn't want *me* to sit on His knee. He was perfect, and I was naughty.

When I learned that we are judged not only by our words and actions, but also by our thoughts, my fate was sealed. Even if I *did* somehow manage to get control of my bad behavior and the unkind words that came out of my mouth, I would still be condemned because of what I was thinking. Bad thoughts popped into my head all the time, but there was nothing I could do about it. The more I tried to make the thoughts go away, the more tenaciously they remained stuck in my head.

The only thing that helped me feel better about myself was receiving praise and admiration, which I sought from any and every source—parents, teachers, friends, acquaintances, and even strangers. I devoted a great deal of time and effort to pleasing others in my attempts to win their approval. Praise was the one thing that pacified my fears and gave me hope that I might someday be good enough.

In the midst of all my worries was the most ominous figure of all—the devil. He was the one responsible for making me think and do so many bad things. He was the dreaded enemy that God and everyone else hated. He made people think it was okay or even fun to sin, but then when you died you didn't get to live happily ever after with God. You had to go down to "you-know-where" and live in outer darkness.

This concept of the devil engendered in me a certain kind of loyalty to God. Even though I didn't love Him, and I was sure He didn't love me, He was my only hope for not having to live with the devil forever after I died.

As I grew older and began participating in firesides, seminary, and youth conferences, I often felt the gentle nudging of the Spirit. Unfortunately, by then I was so deeply entrenched in self-condemnation and the certainty of God's rejection that I didn't nurture those feelings, even when the Spirit lingered with them at the very doorway of my heart.

Just before entering my teen years, I discovered something that seemed to bring me even greater happiness than praise did—attention from boys! I loved it. I craved it. I thrived on it. To gain this attention, I was willing to risk both my good grades and my spotless reputation. With it, life was beautiful. Without it, I was miserable.

As I observed the dating world, I became acutely aware that the girls who claimed the attention of the cutest, most popular guys were usually the skinny ones. I was convinced that if I could just lose enough weight, I would receive the attention I desired, and *then* I would be blissfully happy. Though I still did my best to merit as much praise as possible, cute guys—and the weight I "needed" to lose to be attractive to them—became my number one focus.

Toward the end of high school, this obsession with body image took me down a path that led to a full blown eating disorder.

When I first discovered that throwing up was an easy way to avoid the consequences of eating too much, I was delighted.

Unfortunately, my discovery quickly turned into a nightly bathroom ritual. Although my resulting weight loss was indeed rewarded with a great deal of male attention, there was a catch: a covert tyrant now ruled my life. The irresistible urge to binge and purge tormented me mercilessly, constantly dominating my thoughts and behavior.

Hiding my eating disorder from my family, college roommates, and others required careful planning and endless deceit. My efforts to prevent anyone from suspecting the truth left me isolated and emotionally exhausted. It also created a million new reasons for God to reject me. As I battled with my double life, I gradually came to believe that my compulsion with food was the source of all my misery.

Though I felt completely unworthy of God's help, I knew of no other place to turn for a remedy to the nightmare I was living. Certainly anyone I told would be totally disgusted and would feel obligated to expose my hideous secret to everyone. Since eating disorders were not a common topic at that time, I thought I was the only one in the world who had this kind of problem.

Each night I begged God to help me overcome this monster and free me of my despair. I tried to demonstrate my sincere humility by telling Him that I knew I was totally worthless and undeserving. At times I wondered if He was testing me to see if I really wanted to change bad enough to deserve His help. Maybe He wanted me to somehow become strong enough on my own to control my impulses.

Each new beginning in my life was a time of great hope whether I was starting a new job, starting a new college semester, or going on a mission. I always promised that I was going to finally leave the old, unworthy Elona behind and become the person God wanted me to be. However, my compulsive behaviors and their accompanying beliefs always tagged along with me, painfully persisting from day to day, month to month, year to year.

I continued to be active in the Church, but I felt like a fraud identifying myself as a Mormon. At one point I talked with my bishop about removing my name from the Church records. He asked me not to be too hasty, and suggested that I keep myself so involved with other things that I didn't have time to overeat. I tried to do what he advised, but my attempts failed as always.

In spite of all my hang-ups, I continued to do well academically. I also became friends with some wonderful people, though I never dared confide in any of them. I was blessed with many spiritual moments during those years, but the haunting fear that I would never measure up to God's lofty standards always hovered close by. Sometimes despair rushed in and flooded my life. Other times it lurked in the shadows, waiting to snuff out any spark of hope that might be ignited.

After I married, my husband's peaceful confidence in the Lord had a calming effect on my fears. They still reared their ugly heads from time to time, but Monte was able to help me abandon my eating disorder, and our first ten years together were eventful and busy. We moved several times as he completed his education, we built our modest dream home, and we brought six beautiful children into the world. These little people were the joy of my existence, but my fears intensified as I worried about the added responsibility I now had of preparing *them* for the celestial kingdom.

As the years went on, I failed miserably at accomplishing all my Molly Mormon mothering goals. Surely it would be my fault if my children weren't good enough, and they never would be at the rate I was going. My life was a wild roller coaster ride, alternating between frequent climbs to joyful heights and countless descents to the depths of despair and depression.

Today I rejoice in my deep love for God, and for His amazing love for each of His children.

My ability to truly rejoice in God's love was preceded by an oppressively dark period. The darkness began instantly when David, our sixteen-year-old son, informed me that he was gay. Sorrow and despair consumed my thoughts as the following days, weeks, and months dragged painfully by. But the darkness ended one day as abruptly as it had begun.

I was on the phone with my walking partner, Marcia, talking about the challenging situation facing our friend Cindy. Her fifteen-year-old son's life was threatened by total kidney failure, and she was planning to give him one of her kidneys the following week. After discussing the risks, the lengthy recovery, and the many needs of the rest of her large family, I commented that Cindy was making a truly incredible sacrifice for her son. "You're absolutely right," Marcia assured me. "There's no question it will be hard for her. But I'd do it for any of my kids, and so would you."

My reply tumbled from my lips without even a hint of hesitation. "I would for anyone but David."

Those uncensored words shocked us both, creating a long and awkward silence. Barely able to utter a good-bye, I dropped the phone and crumpled to the floor as my thoughtless words reverberated loudly—accusingly—in my head.

I would for anyone but David. I would for anyone but David.

A sob caught in my throat, and bitter tears sprang to my eyes as the implications of my words churned in my mind. Was I indeed the heartless mother they proclaimed me to be? Was it possible that I honestly had no affection for this son who had once meant the world to me? Even though I thought it was his fault that my life was in such shambles, would I really choose to let him die? From the depths of my broken heart came a truly wretched cry.

"Heavenly Father, please don't let me be a coldhearted mother!"

What happened next is difficult, if not impossible, for me to describe. One moment I was sitting on the floor, overwhelmed with grief, and the next moment, my mind was engaged in a distinct conversation with the Divine unlike anything I had ever experienced.

First, I was tenderly informed that I was not a coldhearted mother. I was so relieved that I wanted to leap to my feet and shout for joy. But that feeling was quickly interrupted as I was gently, yet firmly, chastised for my lack of compassion.

"But what about your son? Isn't he suffering too? He has no family, no friends, no Church members supporting him like you do."

As the truth of those words sank into my heart, the anguish of my own pain was swallowed up by an urgency to ease my son's staggering burden.

"But, Heavenly Father," I cried aloud, "What can I do? I don't understand enough about homosexuality to be a good mother for him!"

God's response was concise and unmistakable. "You don't have to understand. *You just have to love.*"

As I contemplated those words, I found myself enveloped in a glorious sea of love and acceptance. During this amazing tutorial, God not only allowed me to experience His unwavering love for me and for my troubled son, but He also taught me that this same divine love is extended to every single one of His children.

In that moment, the healing power of God's infinite love flooded over and through every part of my being, releasing all of the fear and heartache that had imprisoned my soul for so many years. Suddenly I felt joyfully free and alive as never before. It was a feeling I wanted to hold on to forever.

This experience initiated a wonderful new era in my life. I had cried out to God from the depths of my broken heart, feeling totally unworthy and hopeless, and I had come away with a joyful heart, overflowing with love and new understanding. Interestingly enough, my circumstances hadn't changed at all. I still had a gay son who skipped school all the time, swore at me whenever he got upset, and stayed out all night. Yet somehow in that moment, Christ swept away all of my fears, along with the worry and pain they had brought with them. He replaced them with peace and joy and hope—not with the expectation that my son would magically change, but with the confidence that we were both in God's loving hands and that He was there to walk this unknown path with us.

Experiencing God's love in this profound way gave me a completely new frame of reference for relating with my son. My heart was filled with deep compassion for this sensitive young man, who had felt such intense rejection on every hand. I was finally ready to be there for him. For many months, the Spirit remained with me, teaching me moment by moment how to offer him love.

I no longer had to bite my tongue to avoid saying anything unkind or disapproving. Such thoughts hardly entered my mind. I was frequently given words to say, and sometimes the guidance and strength to say nothing at all. David didn't always like how I handled our interactions, but even when he yelled and cursed at me, my spirit remained calm and loving. God had given me the counsel to love my son, and He was giving me the constant guidance and ability to actually do it.

That pivotal encounter with God—which I have come to refer to as "my change of heart experience"—completely transformed the way I felt about Him. The shackles of my fearful beliefs lay broken and powerless at my feet, along with my Molly Mormon perfectionism. My newfound love for God, and His amazing love for me, became the foundation of my life.

As I revisited scripture stories that had once bothered me, I understood them in a totally different light. Even when the reasons behind God's commandments or actions weren't clear to me, I knew in my soul that *everything* God says or does is grounded in His perfect love for His children.

The peace and happiness in my life seemed almost too good to be true. In the morning, I woke up rejoicing in my new relationship with God. At night I went to bed with a heart full of gratitude for the abundance of love in my life. What had once been a nightly routine of tearful self-condemnation vanished as the habit of harshly judging myself and others melted away. Throughout the day, I often recognized God's guidance as He showed me how to share His love with everyone around me.

At times I was tempted to reclaim my worries about David's future or the impact his behavior might have on our family. Whenever that happened, I reminded myself that I'd given those concerns to God so I could get on with the business of loving. Even though the old Molly Mormon arguments about needing to be in control were sometimes compelling, I wasn't about to exchange my freedom and joy for the overwhelming heartache I had left at God's feet.

Many times I have reflected on that precious experience and the profound impact it had on my life. Without doubt, I experienced what Elder Oaks calls "the greatest miracle"—*a change of heart.*[4] My heart, which had long been paralyzed with fear and pain, was now filled with love, hope, and peace. Instead of anxiously trying to avoid the wrath of some mysterious, condemning being, I realized I had a generous, devoted, personal companion who was ready to stand by me through all of life's ups and downs. I felt boundless love and loyalty for this merciful God, who had revealed His true nature to me.

With this change of heart, my happiness no longer depended on my ability to impress others or to manipulate them into loving me. I didn't have to wait for the praise of man to make me happy. My happiness came from God. His love and confidence flowed effortlessly to me and from me. I saw all of my relationships with new eyes, and I rejoiced in the freedom and pleasure my new perspective brought me. My greatest desire was to continue to feel God's presence in my life.

For a long time, whenever I reflected back on that amazing day, I felt a resurgence of pure love. God's love was there for me each time David called to vent about the latest challenges in his life. Even though I didn't always understand his feelings or his choices, I continued to feel a joyful, unreserved love for him.

After a few years, however, I began to notice that I was no longer responding to David from a place of pure love. For some reason, recalling my change of heart experience had lost some of its power. I continued to treat David kindly, but rather than feeling love flow freely from my heart, I found myself consciously choosing—sometimes even forcing—my loving behavior. In spite of my sincere desire to retain it, the *brightness* of my wonderful change of heart had slipped from my grasp.

Looking back, I believe God was teaching me an important truth regarding a change of heart. It's easy to get the impression that a change of heart is a single event, similar to flipping on a light switch—where there was once darkness, suddenly there is now light. That can be true in some cases as it was for the Apostle Paul, for Alma the Younger, and even for me. Following my change of heart experience, I did enjoy a beautiful period of unrestrained love and light. But eventually, I realized that it was clearly not a gift I could receive in a moment and then simply possess forever.

There is evidence that Alma understood what I was in the process of learning. In the midst of a string of probing questions he asked, "If ye have experienced a change of heart, and if ye have felt to sing the song of redeeming love, I would ask, *can ye feel so now?*"[5] He understood that just as a light bulb must stay connected to its source of electrical power to remain illuminated, a changed heart has to remain firmly connected to God's love, the source of all spiritual power, or it will lose its motivating, enlivening brightness.

I truly *wanted* to hold on to the brightness of my change of heart which had filled my life with unfettered love, but desire alone was obviously not enough. I needed to learn how to stay connected (or to continually reconnect) with the motivating joy of God's love. Otherwise I would never be able to keep Molly Mormon at bay. Fortunately that grand adventure awaited me a few years in the future.

2

THE IRON ROD AS A WEAPON OF SELF-DESTRUCTION

*Using the Scriptures to Help Me
Keep My Change of Heart*

I confess that I resented the scriptures.

When I was young, few people carried their scriptures to church with them. Many families didn't even have a complete set of scriptures in their homes. My dad kept his black leather Bible and triple combination safely out of reach on an upper shelf in our living room. We weren't allowed to touch them unless he was sitting next to us on the couch. Though Daddy's regard for the scriptures was obvious, to my young mind, they were mysterious and intimidating. The language was strange, and the delicate pages were filled with countless rules you had to follow if you wanted to get into the celestial kingdom.

I remember being taught a series of Sunday School lessons about the ten commandments with all the "thou shalt not" rules. Thou shalt not lie. Thou shalt not steal. Thou shalt not wish for what other people have. I was busted on all accounts!

Furthermore, there were all of those stories about God's anger and the destruction He caused when people didn't obey Him. Maybe really wicked people deserved to die, but what about the little children who drowned when Noah's family floated off in the ark? That was so unfair, and it surely had to be terrifying for them.

And what about Lot's wife? Why would God change someone into a pillar of salt just because she turned around to look at her house? That punishment didn't seem to fit the crime at all.

Because I continued to view scripture stories and teachings through my distorted lens of fear, I was adeptly wielding the iron rod as a weapon of self-destruction long before I reached adulthood. Each commandment provided me with another opportunity to notice that I was falling pathetically short of perfection. Instead of allowing the words of God to bring heavenly comfort to my earthly existence, I used them to create my own living hell.

By the time I began considering a mission, the general authorities were emphasizing personal scripture study. They encouraged adults to purchase their own copies of the scriptures and take them to all church meetings. It was common to hear talks about how we should read the scriptures for thirty minutes a day. That counsel always came with the promise that if we followed it, we would feel closer to God, strengthen our families, and receive heaven's guidance to solve our problems.

For me, though, the scriptures felt more like the problem than the solution. I felt guilty because I didn't find them interesting, and when others taught from the scriptures, I was reminded over and over that I was hopelessly undeserving of God's blessings. Other people testified of ways that scripture study had helped them, but I couldn't let go of my guilt and fear long enough to let the Spirit show me how the scriptures could help *me*. Instead of loving the scriptures like I knew I "should," I resented them for adding more stress to my life.

My husband has always loved the scriptures. When we first met at BYU, he studied them every morning before class. Later, when we were newlyweds and he was working a custodial shift requiring him to clock-in at 4:00 a.m., he still got up early enough to study the scriptures before leaving for work.

A few years into our marriage, he made an extensive study of temple worship, using the scriptures and a variety of other resources. Sometime later, he used Greek and Hebrew dictionaries to increase his understanding of scriptural language. I admired his diligence and enjoyed the insights he shared with me, but my fearful Molly Mormon thinking always led me back to feeling guilty and inadequate rather than uplifted and inspired.

One Sunday afternoon, after yet another lesson in Relief Society about the importance of scripture study, I turned to my husband and flatly declared, "I'm never going to make it to the celestial kingdom. I might as well give up and accept it right now, so my life doesn't have to be so miserable and stressful. I'm always trying to change, but I can't make myself do everything I'm supposed to. There is absolutely no way I'm ever going to make it."

Familiar with my roller-coaster emotions, my husband calmly asked, "How can you be so sure that you're not going to make it?"

Then I stated what had become increasingly obvious to me over the years. "I'm never going to make it, because no matter how hard I try, I simply cannot force myself to read the scriptures for thirty minutes every day."

My husband looked at me in amusement and then thoughtfully replied, "Show me where it says in the scriptures—or anywhere else, for that matter—that you can't get into the celestial kingdom if you haven't read the scriptures for thirty minutes a day."

His challenge momentarily interrupted my ranting, because when I stopped to think about it, I knew the scriptures didn't spell out scripture study in exactly those terms. But still I forged on. "Well, all of the General Authorities say it's important to read the scriptures for thirty minutes a day, and I simply *cannot* do it. Even when I do pretty well for a while, I always mess up again. There's absolutely no way I'm ever going to make it!"

Later I admitted to myself that there was probably no one in the whole world—not even the prophet—who had actually read the scriptures for thirty minutes every single day. That meant, according to my logic, that the celestial kingdom was destined to be empty. Of course, I didn't believe that would be the case, but debunking my faulty logic didn't change my despair over the matter. It actually kind of irritated me because it meant I had to keep wrestling with guilt and resentment, when giving up would have been so much easier.

After years of continued struggle, my change of heart experience brought a beautiful new attitude toward the scriptures. Finally I was able to view them as words of encouragement rather than words of condemnation. Their warnings became words of love rather than angry threats. I realized that the scriptures were designed to help me avoid pain and suffering, and to show me how to joyfully receive the companionship of the Spirit.

From then on, when speakers or teachers discussed specific references at church, I enjoyed following along, making notes and marking verses that resonated with my heart. Occasionally I tried to establish a consistent routine of personal scripture study, but my attempts were always short-lived, foiled each time by my lack of self-discipline.

As I explained earlier, the memory of my wonderful change of heart experience carried me for a long time, but then it gradually began to lose its power to lift me above my natural woman tendencies. For some reason I couldn't seem to hang onto it no matter how much I wanted to. Though the assurance of God's love always remained with me, the *brightness* of my change of heart had dimmed and I was left yearning for that feeling of closeness with God I had enjoyed.

Over the next several years, our children graduated from high school and left home for college, missions, and marriage. I continued to treasure the freedom I felt from the constant fear of failure, but I knew an even richer life was available if I could only reconnect more completely with God's love. I had a sense that the scriptures were the missing link, but how to make myself study them remained a mystery.

I often talked with my sister about my unsuccessful efforts to establish a habit of daily scripture study. Like me, she wanted to study the scriptures regularly, but she couldn't make it happen either. Together we lamented the lack of self-discipline that kept us from enjoying a closer relationship with God.

Today I rejoice and *rejoice* in the gift of the scriptures!

In early 2001, my sister called and excitedly shared some of her experiences with a twelve-step program based on The Book of Mormon. She said the program was explained in a book by Colleen Harrison called *He Did Deliver Me from Bondage.*[1] The title instantly commanded my attention, and I eagerly anticipated her further explanation. My sister admitted that she'd been using the book, actually a kind of workbook, for several months. But she had delayed telling me about it because the results had at first seemed too good to be true.

Now I was really listening!

She said that the program required only fifteen minutes of focused study each day, but the stories of how it had touched her spirit and opened her heart to God's love, guidance, and inspiration were electrifying. She was living what I had experienced following my change of heart, and I couldn't wait to get my hands on the program.

Finding a copy of the book was no easy task. All the bookstores I called either didn't carry it, or they were out. However, after a series of persistent phone calls that culminated in an evening trip to a distributor's home, I finally obtained my prize.

Early the next morning, I sat down with my scriptures and my new book before me. I was ready to begin.

After reading the lengthy foreword and preface, I turned the page and found it entirely blank except for a single verse of scripture:

> But behold, he did deliver them because they did humble themselves before him; and because they cried mightily unto him he did deliver them out of bondage; and thus doth the Lord work with his power in all cases among the children of men, extending the arm of mercy toward them that put their trust in him.[2]

As I read those words, the Spirit witnessed to my heart that they held a very important, very personal message for me. I obviously wasn't in the same kind of bondage I had known during the desperate years of my eating disorder, so what was the Lord trying to tell me? I was sitting at that table because

I hungered for the divine connection which had once allowed me to love unconditionally. Could this book be the key to recovering that amazing gift?

The introductory discussion said I should "awake and arouse [my] faculties," "experiment upon [His] words," and "exercise a particle of faith."[3] Well, my faculties had been awakened and aroused, and I was downright antsy to enter the scripture study laboratory.

The author said that the required lab materials included the scriptures, a notebook, and a pen. She explained that each fifteen minutes of daily experimentation would include praying, reading, and writing. I guess she figured everyone would understand what she meant by praying and reading, but to clarify the writing part she referred to a page in the appendix titled "What Is Capturing?"

According to her, *capturing* meant to really get a hold on something and make it your own. She said it was essential to capture each assigned scripture passage by underlining, copying, and making notes of the ideas that stand out to you. The critical final step was to write down whatever thoughts came to your mind as you pondered those ideas and asked yourself questions. Then she gave a list of sample questions you could ask.

"Why is this important to you?"

"How does it connect for you?"

"What does it say to you?"

"How do you see this applying to your life?"

"What does God want you to understand from this scripture today?"

She went on to say that for her, *capturing* often turned into a prayer, and that as she wrote, she frequently noticed the voice of the Lord speaking to her mind and her heart.

As I considered her words, I faltered. What if nothing came to mind for me to write? What if I was setting myself up for another failure? Maybe I was asking too much of this book. Suddenly it all seemed too unsettling, and for a moment, I was tempted to play it safe and set the book aside.

However, as I recalled my sister's enthusiastic testimonial, I was infused with a compelling burst of new hope. I had to at least give the experiment a *try*. After all, it only required fifteen minutes a day, and what if it actually worked? What if this program could somehow lead me to the connection with God that I was longing for?

For seven days, I got up early each morning, said a prayer, and then opened my scriptures. The verses I captured that first week focused on the weakness of the natural woman and her need to rely on God. It wasn't hard for me to see how these applied to me. I liked being directed to a specific scripture passage each day, and I liked having a designated amount of time to ponder and write about it.

The chapter for the second week focused on Christ's redeeming power. As I began to write my thoughts and feelings about the tender, intimate messages contained in the assigned verses, a familiar Spirit gently crept into my heart. It was the same amazing feeling of love and peace and comfort that had healed my broken heart years earlier.

I was immediately hooked! Early morning scripture study became my favorite part of the day. I found myself extending my study time to an hour, and sometimes more. Day after day, the feeling of pure love would sneak up on me, and I would be left catching my spiritual breath, awed and humbled by its recurring presence. An overwhelming sense of gratitude filled my life as that beautiful, unrestrained love once again flowed into my heart and then out to others. The brightness of my change of heart had returned. God's irresistible love was making me joyful and whole, moment by moment, just as it had before.

Each morning my eyes popped open before my alarm sounded, and I hurried to my scriptures, eager to begin the day with God. A few times I read an entire chapter and did all the writing assignments in a single day. There was no thought of "forcing" or "disciplining myself" to study the scriptures. I had discovered a beautiful fountain of living water that quenched my spiritual thirst, and all I wanted to do was sit and drink from it. In the words of President Hinckley, my scripture time became "something far more enjoyable than a duty; ... it [became] a love affair with the word of God."[4] As the days rolled by it became clear that the scriptures truly were my doorway to God's love, and I had finally found the key.

I frequently recognized the Spirit's influence guiding my choices and directing me away from fearful or unkind thinking. My prayers became more focused and meaningful. This method of studying the scriptures led me to all that I had been looking for and even more. Not only was I feeling God's love every day, I was developing my ability to use the scriptures as a means of *inviting* Him into my life every day. At last I had learned how to "turn on the light switch," and I was thrilled to be doing my part to maintain the connection.

When I started working through the final chapter of the book, I worried that I might lose my spiritual connection if I didn't have the author's questions and comments to guide my studies. However, I soon realized that I didn't have to be a gifted writer like Colleen Harrison, or a capable scriptorian like my husband to find treasures in the scriptures. It didn't matter that I couldn't remember specific references or all of the details of a certain story. I simply needed to show up, open my scriptures, read, ponder and write. When I made the effort, the Spirit always attended my feasting.

From time to time, I hear the quote, "If you want to talk to God, pray. If you want God to talk to you, read the scriptures." I have joyfully experienced the reality of that truth, but I would tweak the second phrase to say, "If I want God to *consistently* talk to me, I need to consistently pray, ponder *and capture* the scriptures."

Of course, that doesn't mean I only feel the Spirit from the scriptures when I write down my thoughts. Sometimes reading a single verse or reflecting on a short phrase floods my soul with the sweetness of God's love. But, capturing—actually writing down my thoughts and feelings—helps me set aside my worldly distractions and focus my full attention on the less obvious, spiritual world. In that frame of mind, I'm better able to tune in to my feelings and desires, and respond to the inner guidance that comes from the Holy Spirit.

Capturing helps me understand myself, it helps me understand God, it helps me feel His amazing love, and it helps me receive personal messages from Him. It increases my ability to embrace my natural woman tendencies and to humbly seek the guidance I need to manage them.

Capturing is a form of pondering or meditating.* It's an enlightening form of prayer. It's a tool I depend on regularly to connect my soul to God.

After I fell in love with the scriptures, my husband reintroduced me to a wonderful tool that had been in our home for years, a computerized scripture program called LDS View.[5] This awesome tool rescues me when I don't know where to find a certain scripture passage. It helps me when I want to research a gospel topic, or study the meaning of scripture words in English, Hebrew, or Greek. In the appendix of this book, I share an example of how I used LDS View one day to study the principle of repentance.

You'll also find details in the appendix about another tool I have come to appreciate. It's a method of seeking guidance by randomly opening the scriptures. Wendy Watson Nelson explains this method and gives several examples of people using it in her book titled *Rock Solid Relationships*.[6]

Although I don't routinely use this method, it has blessed me more than once in a time of great need. I'm convinced that God generously placed this tool in my path because He is eager for me to resolve conflicts as quickly as possible and enjoy loving relationships with those around me.

Learning about New Testament culture has likewise blessed me in my quest to receive messages from the scriptures. Monte started sharing insights with me from his reading about Middle Eastern culture several years ago, but when I asked to see his books, their techy format and language put me off. However,

---

* President McKay said, "Meditation is the language of the soul. Meditation is a form of prayer. ... Meditation is one of the most secret, most sacred doors through which we pass into the presence of the Lord." (See complete quote and reference in appendix.)

as I continued to consider Bible stories from the confines of my own cultural experience, I kept wondering what I was missing. Eventually I got brave enough to venture into those intimidating pages. I haven't yet read any of Monte's culture books from cover to cover, and I most likely never will, but each time I study from them, I receive new insights into the depths of the Savior's wisdom and compassion.

At the risk of committing a serious injustice because of my brevity, I'll share an example from the story of the prodigal son. In the scriptures we are told that the younger of two sons goes to his father and asks for his part of the family wealth. After the father honors his request, the son goes to a foreign country and wastes his fortune in "riotous living." He finds work feeding pigs, but his circumstances are so dire that he wishes he could eat the pigs' food. He finally decides to return to his father's house, acknowledge his unworthiness, and ask to be employed as a servant.

When the son "was yet a great way off, his father saw him, and had compassion, and ran, and fell on his neck, and kissed him."[7] These few words create a tender scene, with beautiful symbolism pointing to Christ's willingness to forgive us and welcome us back when we repent.

However, in *The Cross and the Prodigal* by Kenneth Bailey,[8] there is a lengthy explanation of the culture and customs which sheds much new light on this parable. Bailey says that whenever someone lost his fortune among the Gentiles as did the prodigal son, a rejection ceremony was enacted the moment anyone saw him returning. The villagers would set a large pot in front of him and smash it, symbolizing that they would have nothing further to do with him. Traditionally the father would remain in his house while this was done, angry at his son for shaming the family. He would only summon the son after requiring him to sit outside for some time. Contrary to cultural expectations, this father ran to greet his son, embraced him, and according to the Greek word for *kissed*, he either kissed him again and again, or he kissed him tenderly.

It's not unusual for me to see older men running along the streets of my neighborhood. Men of all ages often jog around our community in exercise shorts. Of course I know that Jewish men wore long robes so I imagined the father hurrying to his son, somewhat encumbered by his clothing. But Bailey's book offers new insight into this detail of the story as well. The Greek word for *run* is the technical word used for a stadium footrace. This footrace came at great cost to the father. In their culture, men over twenty-five didn't ever run. A householder of the father's advanced age always walked in a slow, dignified manner. To race, he would have to take the front edge of his robe in his hand and expose his legs. Such an act was considered most shameful and humiliating.

The people on the street would be so amazed by this unusual scene that they would be distracted from tormenting the son and would instead run after the father who was publically shaming himself. Bailey comments, "It is his compassion that leads the father to race out to his son. He knows what his son will face in the village. He takes upon himself the shame and humiliation due the prodigal."[9]

As I ponder the symbolism in the story from this perspective, my understanding is expanded and my appreciation for the Savior deepens. He doesn't just offer forgiveness. He is eager to rush in and protect me from my own follies, regardless of the cost to himself. He's willing to suffer my consequences so

I don't have to. The father's behavior is a beautiful symbol for Christ's atoning sacrifice.

Many other details are included in Bailey's explanation that I won't go into here, but I love pondering them. They enrich my understanding of the nature of Christ's love. Every time I open one of these books, new light is shed on stories and concepts I have read and heard all my life.

Today I recognize the scriptures as a truly beautiful manifestation of God's eternal love for His children, instead of some kind of ominous taskmaster. Pondering the messages they hold for me has become a frequent and joyful part of my life. I love the statement Colleen Harrison shared in her book that says, "I put God first in my life by putting God first in my day."

But even so, there are still times when I don't open my scriptures first thing in the morning, and sometimes I don't get to them at all during the day. When that happens, regardless of the reason, I'm no longer afraid that God is mad at me or that He is eagerly waiting to punish me for my negligence. He knows me. He knows my heart. He knows my nature. He loves me unconditionally even with all my mess-ups.

And oh, how I love Him!

When I don't study my scriptures early in the day, I usually have the lingering feeling that I'm missing something. At the end of such days, when I kneel for my personal prayer, I'm drawn to open my scriptures, even if only for a couple of minutes. Sometimes I pick them up and press them to my heart, grateful that whether I read them for a minute or study them for an hour, God's love radiates to me from them. His words anchor my life. They offer me peace and guidance. Whenever I feel myself removed from the Spirit, I can usually close the gap by prayerfully opening those sacred pages, pondering their words, and writing whatever comes to mind.

President Kimball said, "Each of us, at some time in our lives, must discover the scriptures for ourselves—and not just discover them once, but rediscover them again and again ... and let them work mightily within us."[10]

Discovering and rediscovering the scriptures continues to be an incredibly joyful journey for me. I truly cherish the scriptures, and I affectionately refer to them as my "love notes from God." In this electronic world of fantasy and virtual reality, the scriptures have the power to create their own kind of amazing "magic." I owe a deep, deep debt of gratitude to the prophets and to all others who have sacrificed so I can have this magic at my fingertips.

The beautiful words of the scriptures have become the fountain I most often drink from in my effort to retain and renew my treasured change of heart.

3

COLD FLOORS AND ACHING KNEES

—— ⟨⟩⟩⟩ ——

Making Prayer a Pleasure

I confess that my prayers were mostly a matter of routine.

When I was a small child, my mother taught me to kneel by my bed and say a prayer before going to sleep. I remember repeating, "Heavenly Father, bless me. Make me a good little girl. Bless Mommy and Daddy. Bless sister and brother. Bless all kind friends. ..." By then, the chill from the hardwood floor was creeping into my legs, and all I wanted to do was jump into bed and get warm.

As time went on, I learned that I was supposed to thank God for all the good things in my life and that I could also ask Him for anything I wanted. However, I wasn't convinced that enduring the cold floor to ask for special favors was worthwhile, because as far as I could tell, my prayers did little more than help me avoid the guilt I felt if I skipped them. I didn't feel any closer to God for having prayed, and I still made a lot of bad choices no matter how many times I asked Him to make me a good little girl. The prayers I heard others say didn't seem to make much difference either. Sick people still died, crops still suffered because of the shortage of irrigation water, and the poor and the needy were still poor and needy.

I quickly learned that there were a lot of rules governing prayer. You were supposed to say personal and family prayers on your knees. You had to bow your head, fold your arms, close your eyes, and hold still during every prayer. You didn't have to say a prayer before eating a little snack, but you had to say a blessing on the food before eating a full meal. If you were the one praying, you weren't supposed to start until everyone was being reverent. At church, the boys saying the sacrament prayers had to kneel down, but other than that, people saying prayers were supposed to stand up. Occasionally someone prayed without standing up, but I never could figure out what rule allowed them to be the exception to the real rule.

One of my pet peeves was General Conference prayers. They were always excessively long and boring, so keeping my eyes closed the whole time was nearly impossible. Even when we were just listening to conference on the radio, we were supposed to stop whatever we were doing to fold our arms and bow our heads whenever prayers came on. If someone said a long prayer in sacrament meeting, my siblings and I would look at each other in disgust and whisper, "That was as long as a *conference* prayer!"

Sometimes at night after family prayer, there would be an exchange that went something like, "Momma, Nikki had her eyes open!" or "Janell was moving around!"

Mother's response was usually, "How do you know? Did you have *your* eyes open?"

The realization that we had tattled on ourselves in the process of tattling on someone else always came a little late, but that wasn't what mattered. What mattered were the *rules*. They were my focus, because they were what I could understand. Talking to an invisible Being didn't really make a lot of sense to me.

Sunday School and Primary teachers also taught us a set of rules they called the four steps of prayer.

1. Address God by saying "Heavenly Father" or "Father in Heaven."
2. Thank God for your many blessings.
3. Ask God for the things you need.
4. End by saying, "In the name of Jesus Christ, Amen."

Those rules were simple and easy to follow. I liked knowing exactly how a prayer was supposed to be said.

Whether I was at church or at home, I listened intently to determine if people were following the rules correctly. Did they get all four steps in? Did they say them in the right order? Knowing these steps came in handy when I was trying to determine the spirituality of the person saying the prayer. One of my teachers helped me refine this measuring stick by telling us that we should always spend more time thanking Heavenly Father for our blessings than asking Him for more.

Everyone opened their prayers by addressing Heavenly Father in one way or another, and they always closed in Christ's name, so in my mind, the question boiled down to whether they remembered to do a lot of thanking before they started asking.

Over and over I caught people praying the "wrong" way. Although a few got it right, many people mixed it all up, randomly asking and thanking and then thanking and asking. Some shamelessly jumped right in with the asking. Because I was usually busy judging, I hardly ever felt the Spirit when people were praying.

Even my own prayers weren't exempt from my judgments. Often I found myself in a quandary when I realized I'd forgotten to say that I was thankful for something important until after I'd moved on to the asking. Should I wait until the next time I prayed so I could follow the rules with exactness? Or should I mess up the order by saying I was thankful for something after I'd started asking? Either way, God might get mad at me.

At some point, I was told that kneeling with your body erect rather than resting your weight on your lower legs was a sign of greater devotion. Somehow that was supposed to show more commitment to God than being relaxed. When I tried that technique, I couldn't help fidgeting because it made my knees and legs hurt. I wondered if tolerating the pain was part of showing God I really wanted His blessings.

I felt distressed when I learned that we were supposed to be having family prayer in the morning as well as in the evening. Nightly prayers fit into our family routine quite nicely, but morning prayers were a big hassle because we were always racing the clock so we wouldn't miss the school bus. Trying to get everyone together for a prayer was so inconvenient! On top of that, I later learned that if I *really* wanted to be spiritual, I had to say a *personal* prayer in the morning too. Although I wanted to be good enough to get into the celestial kingdom, all that praying seemed like overkill.

The habit of saying my personal prayers at night stuck with me throughout the years, though I never felt they made much difference. Answers were so elusive. Hearing stories about other people's prayers being immediately answered was sometimes heartwarming, but it was also frustrating. Why couldn't I have my own great prayer stories to tell? Oh, right! I wasn't yet good enough for God to favor me like that.

I admit that as a young adult I did receive a couple of definite answers to my prayers. After praying for a few months about going on a mission, I felt a strong assurance that I should go. When I prayed about marrying Monte after my mission, the answer was again unmistakable. These answers helped me move forward in my life, but my confidence in receiving answers was still overshadowed by my fears.

Most often I didn't recognize that the changes happening in my life were actually answers to prayer. For example, when the bingeing and purging of my eating disorder finally ended, I didn't see this change as an answer to my years of pleading with God. I attributed it to the support of my new husband, my demanding new work schedule, and the exhaustion of pregnancy. In hindsight, I can see the Lord's hand in resolving many of the challenges I prayed about. At the time, though, I didn't understand that answers often come subtly in ordinary, everyday ways.

After I got married, I felt a strong desire to increase my spirituality. Committing to begin each day with a personal prayer seemed like the best place to start. Unfortunately I was immediately in the throes—or you could say "the throw-ups"—of morning sickness. My prayers were usually brief to nonexistent as I struggled to drag myself out of bed and get to work on time.

The battle to say a morning prayer continued over the next several years, until I finally hit upon the perfect strategy. I absolutely would not allow myself to make my bed until after I had said my prayers. Since having an unmade bed drove me crazy, my new rule was effective in helping me check morning prayers off my daily list. If for some odd reason I got into my day without making my bed, as soon as I noticed it, I would drop to one knee and direct a few words to God before pulling up the covers.

Finally I was strictly obeying all the rules: I was saying my family and personal prayers on my knees, every morning and evening, and I was dutifully following the four steps of prayer. So why wasn't I feeling more connected to God?

The sad truth was that even though I was carefully following all the rules, I didn't *enjoy* praying. I didn't feel *drawn* to pray. I didn't yet know that God loved me and cared about my life in a personal way. I had no concept of the joyful, intimate relationship He intended for me to share with Him. I still believed He was waiting to see if I was going to mess everything up, or if, by some unlikely fluke, I would somehow, someday, pull my life together and be good enough to deserve His celestial glory.

The day our son told me He was gay felt like the clincher. God would never welcome me into His presence because I had totally failed Him in the most important responsibility of all—motherhood. Even if He did want me to keep praying, what could I ask for that might possibly fix what was wrong? Although I continued to kneel by my bed each night, words escaped me. My mind would spin in ever-darkening circles until I finally gave up and tearfully climbed into bed.

As I lay there in complete despair, the words of a Primary song would drift into my mind:

> Heavenly Father, are you really there?
> And do you hear and answer every child's prayer?
> Some say that heaven is far away,
> But I feel it close around me as I pray.

When I got to that point in the song, grief always overwhelmed me and I wept bitterly. Those words could not have felt more untrue to me. Where was God when I needed Him so desperately?

Eventually the words to the second verse would begin:

> Pray, he is there;
> Speak, he is list'ning.
> You are his child;
> His love now surrounds you.
> He hears your prayer;
> He loves the children.[1]

As those words flowed through my mind, a glimmer of hope would knock at the door of my heart. How I longed to reach out and embrace that hope, but the song seemed so full of cruel deception. God didn't hear my prayers. I didn't feel His love. What I felt was pain. My son was gay. Our family would never be a "forever family." There was nothing God or anyone else could do to make my life match my Molly Mormon definition of perfection.

Today I rejoice in the strength and peace that prayer brings to my life.

Rules and formalities were completely forgotten the day I collapsed beside my bed and begged God to save me from the crushing pain that consumed me. All I could do was cry out to Him from the depths of my anguished soul. His tender response was an outpouring of love and enlightenment unlike anything I had ever experienced or even imagined.

Alma the Younger concisely described my own feelings when he said, "There could be nothing so exquisite and so bitter as were my pains. ... On the other hand, there can be nothing so exquisite and sweet as was my joy."[2] That was *exactly* how I felt.

In my moment of deepest despair, God didn't say, "I really can't help you, Elona. You didn't follow the proper steps of prayer, and besides, you're not kneeling the right way." Instead, as I sat on the floor, feeling totally lost and broken, He raced to my rescue, revealing to me more truth about prayer and about His loving nature than I had learned in all the previous years of my life.

He showed me that the rules and steps of prayer are only a means to an end. They are outward tools that may be useful in bringing me to the doorway of communion with God, but they do not guarantee a divine connection. It's not the order of my words or my posture that make the difference. It's the condition of my heart.

Through my sweet encounter with God, I also learned that prayer isn't a shortcut for changing the circumstances of my life, but rather a way to change the condition of my heart so I can live in hope and rejoicing, regardless of my circumstances. My desperate plea that day was not for God to fix my son so I could be happy, but only that God would somehow relieve my unbearable pain. At last I was ready to allow God to do *His* work *His* way, and His solution to my problem was a mighty change of heart.

Because of my change of heart, prayer is no longer just a matter of routine for me. It's a divine gift, a treasured tool, a welcome means of reconnecting my soul with God and restoring my eternal perspective. Prayer is the bridge between my fearful natural woman who wants a divine Santa Claus to step in and fix everything, and my enlightened, spiritual woman who adores and trusts God. Prayer helps me repent—that is, it helps me return my focus to Christ. He rewards my sincere (though sometimes feeble) efforts by filling my soul with His love and giving me the courage to embrace reality so I can live joyfully.

I used to be afraid that God wouldn't think I was sincere enough if I didn't remember to ask for a desired blessing every single time I prayed, but I don't worry about that anymore. Nor do I fear that He might be mad at me for omitting something I *could* have thanked Him for. I know now that He's not constantly looking for a reason to condemn me. He is there to sustain me. He is eager for me to receive His mercy, grace, and love. He wants me to know that I can trust Him in *all* things. The Spirit repeatedly confirms to my soul that God accepts my grateful rejoicing and that He is tenderly aware of my yearnings and heartaches.

I've come to understand that God counsels me to "pray always" not because He wants to micromanage my life, but because He wants me to remember *He's always there for me*. He offers prayer as my first line of defense against anything that might diminish my joy or restrict my spiritual freedom. When a challenging situation pops up, the circumstances don't always allow me to pause, open my scriptures, and seek the strength and guidance they have to offer. However, I can *always* turn to God and send up an earnest, silent prayer.

My most enjoyable prayers are usually prayers of gratitude and praise. Sometimes, my heart feels like it's going to burst with thankfulness. Those feelings may come as I'm watching my little granddaughters somersault down a hill, or when I'm reflecting on a tender moment shared with a friend. They may come when I'm savoring the sweetness of repentance and forgiveness, or when I'm standing in awe as a glorious dawn paints the early morning sky. I may be doing one of a million lovely things when a sudden urge invites me to pause and verbalize to God the magnitude of my appreciation and my joy.

Whether I kneel and say a formal prayer or just glance heavenward to express my thanks, I love how those moments draw me closer to God. Whenever I find myself feeling somehow removed from Him, a prayer of gratitude is the first tool I look to for closing the gap.

After I started renewing my connection with God each morning through scripture study, I realized I needed to find a more private place to say my personal prayers. Monte and I had always said our individual prayers beside our bed, but sometimes I needed to pray out loud to stay focused, and sometimes my prayers were pretty informal. It was obvious I needed to find a "closet" so I could be alone with God.

First I tried kneeling at our living room window. It was awesome to watch the first light of morning break over the mountain as I prepared to pray, but every sound I heard made me wonder if someone was approaching. Next I tried praying in a more private room in the basement, but before I even got to the stairs, I'd be sidetracked by some task I noticed waiting to be done. Finally I settled on the office. It was right next to our bedroom, but when I shut the door it felt reasonably secluded. That the office window also faced the morning sun was a nice bonus.

Putting some of my favorite pictures of Christ around the room helped to create the ambiance I needed for my new purpose. On one wall, I see myself sitting at Jesus' feet near Jacob's well as He offers His living water. On another wall, He pleads with me to accept His sacrifice in Gethsemane. As I kneel, I can see him walking with me through the fiery furnace. On the wall next to the door He steps from the garden tomb, gazing steadfastly upward, encouraging me to likewise look to the Father in all things. The office has become my Sacred Grove, surely in part because of these beautiful pictures, but more significantly, because of the countless times I have felt God's presence there.

Most often I begin my prayers in a traditional kneeling position with my eyes closed, but as I begin to express gratitude or concerns, my body automatically joins in the experience. Sometimes my arms stretch outward as I savor the feeling of being completely immersed in God's love. Sometimes they reach upward like a little child seeking to be drawn into the comforting embrace of a parent.

On occasion my head tilts back, and the image of love and light spilling onto my face and down over my entire body fills my heart with joy. Sometimes I lean forward until my elbows rest on the floor and my hands extend before me. I can almost feel the blessings splashing into them like a cascading waterfall.

When I'm praying and a specific idea pops into my head, I'll sometimes open my eyes, grab a pen, and jot down my thoughts. If I need to record something in greater detail, I'll jump up and take a seat at my desk or computer. Those kinds of prayers are particularly exciting to me.

Many times after I finish the words of my prayer, I stay on the floor and reflect on the events of the day or the feelings in my heart. I may even lie on my back. A sense of God's goodness washes over me and my heart sends out a simple, joyous offering of gratitude. Sometimes I break into a song of praise. That's when I really need privacy!

One of my morning prayers gave me an unexpected insight into a wonderful characteristic of God. It was a day when things had piled onto my calendar with total disregard for what was already scheduled there. As I knelt, I wondered how I would ever fit all of the high-priority items into the available hours, let alone the ones that seemed less critical. Just thinking about it was exhausting.

"Heavenly Father," I began. "I know I usually ask you to guide me to do whatever *You* need me to do during the day, but today I have so many commitments, I don't see how I could possibly fit in one more thing." I don't remember all of the words I used in my attempt to explain that I really appreciated His guidance, but that in this particular case, I didn't want Him to further complicate my already complicated day. Suddenly my thoughts were interrupted by a feeling of divine delight surrounding me. It was as if I could hear God chuckling, and I instantly understood that my words were the reason for His merriment.

As I considered what I had just said, I smiled sheepishly and then joined in the laughter. What had I been thinking? How did I ever suppose I was going to maintain my sanity throughout this crazy day without the direction of His Holy Spirit? After taking time to savor that precious moment, I again bowed my head, but this time I simply asked God to stay with me throughout the day and to help me understand and do His will. Then I watched in wonder as my day unfolded.

Within the first hour, two people called and cancelled appointments. A couple of other things that I had anticipated would be very time consuming ended up taking hardly any time at all.

In the early afternoon the idea came to me that I should visit a ward member who was recovering in a care center some distance away. For several days I had been hoping to go see her, but I hadn't been able to arrange my schedule so I could make the trip. Little did I know that the way would be opened when I least expected it.

After a lovely visit I still had time to meet my last afternoon commitment, which also turned out to be unexpectedly short. When I got home I relaxed for a few minutes before preparing dinner for my family. I even had time to eat with them before going to my evening meeting.

That night as I closed the office door and knelt to thank God for the amazing way He had orchestrated my day, my thoughts returned to my morning prayer. With a smile on my face and a heart full of joy, I thanked Him for the blessings He had showered over me, and especially for the opportunity to experience His delightful sense of humor.

Looking back on my life, I realize that God has always been mindful of me, even though I thought that most of my prayers went unanswered. Even when I did recognize moments of spiritual tenderness or enlightenment, my misunderstanding of His true nature prevented me from receiving the peace and joy He wanted for me.

Today I can see that prayer, both formal and informal, is a powerful defense against my fearful Molly Mormon tendencies. It has become a treasured, spiritual lifeline instead of a duty I must perform to appease an angry God.

Most of the time now, I'm *joyously* drawn to pray. Of course I go through ups and downs. Occasionally I get a bit cantankerous and I don't feel like praying at all. However, I no longer doubt God's love or His willingness—indeed, His great desire—to be involved in the details of my life. I know He's eager to bless me. It brings me unspeakable joy when I come to Him and feel I am truly in His presence.

4

YOU CAN WATCH *JOHNNY LINGO* ONLY SO MANY TIMES

Allowing the Sabbath to Fulfill Its Divine Purpose

I confess that I dreaded Sundays.

As a small child, I looked forward to Sundays because it was the only day of the week I had the chance to play with friends. We lived on a farm a few miles out of town, and my friends might as well have lived a hundred miles away. Most parents didn't spend their time or resources running kids here and there just to play. Mine certainly didn't. However, when I was young, Sunday School was held in the morning, and sacrament meeting was held in the evening. This schedule provided the perfect arrangement for playing with friends. Without requiring anything extra of our parents, we could go home with a friend after Sunday School, play during the afternoon hours, and then go back home with our own families after sacrament meeting. I loved it!

As I got a little older, I continued to enjoy socializing on Sunday, but from what I was being taught, both at church and around the dinner table, I began to realize that there were a whole lot of Sunday rules I needed to follow. Since I wanted to get into the celestial kingdom someday, I was anxious to get all those rules in my head so God wouldn't be mad at me for accidently breaking one. Besides, knowing all of the rules helped me impress my teachers and win their praise.

Thus, the Sabbath nitpicking began.

If you were a good Mormon, you had to attend church both morning and evening, every Sunday. The only possible exception was if you were *really* sick, and even then you had to be more dead than alive to stay home if you still wanted to be counted among the truly faithful. Another hard-and-fast rule was no shopping on Sunday. That wasn't really an issue, as everything in our town was closed on Sunday except the bar, and of course *that* would never be a temptation for a nitpicker.

We had frequent debates about whether watching TV on the Sabbath was wrong, and if it was wrong, did it become less wrong or even a *good* thing if you watched a show with the whole family? Most people agreed that hunting or fishing broke the Sabbath. Some even argued that you weren't keeping the Sabbath day holy if you went for a drive up the canyon.

Another area of disagreement was over food preparation for Sunday dinner. Some thought the meal should be kept simple, while others thought that a lot of extra effort was appropriate, because Sunday dinner was the highlight of the week for their family. Cleaning up after meals was fine, but vacuuming or scrubbing a floor was not acceptable. A lot of home chores were strictly off limits. Doing laundry was especially considered a Sabbath breaker because those were the days of wringer washers and outside clotheslines.

Although sewing was a valued skill, you weren't supposed to sew *anything* on Sunday. That included using a sewing machine as well as hand stitching, crocheting, knitting, and whatever else. More than once, my mother's friend told us that every stitch we put in on the Sabbath would have to be picked out in heaven with our noses. I kind of assumed she was teasing, but I still felt guilty if I had to sew on a button or mend a seam so I'd have something to wear to church. Ironing white shirts for my dad and my brother on Sunday morning caused me a mountain of guilt.

Not working on Sunday was kind of a tricky commandment for farmers. Cows still had to be milked, and animals needed to be fed, regardless of the day. But for anything beyond the absolute necessities, my parents deferred to the-ox-in-the-mire principle. When the Pharisees reprimanded Christ for healing on the Sabbath, He responded, "Which of you shall have an ass or an ox fallen into a pit, and will not straightway pull him out on the sabbath day?"[1]

Mother often said, "It's okay to pull the ox out of the mire on Sunday, as long as you didn't push it in on Saturday." That left us discussing all kinds of hypothetical scenarios, trying to determine which situations constituted a legitimate ox in the mire and which ones would be a violation of the Sabbath.

If you got a flat tire on Sunday, it was okay to change it on Sunday. But if you knew the tire was flat on Saturday, you broke the Sabbath if you changed it on Sunday.

If a farmer knew he had a fence that needed to be repaired but went fishing on Saturday instead of taking care of it, he was breaking the Sabbath if he fixed the fence on Sunday.

On the other hand, if the farmer's animals broke through the fence on Sunday, it was okay for the farmer to repair it on Sunday.

I don't remember any talk about seeking the Spirit to help determine an appropriate course of action in any of those discussions, although it could have been mentioned every single time. I was probably too rule-oriented to consider such an option.

For my parents, Sunday usually meant nice, long afternoon naps while kids played at home or visited friends. Sometimes after their naps, they played backyard baseball with us. It was so much fun that I was pretty sure we were breaking the Sabbath. The same was true of game playing after our evening sacrament meetings. I loved playing Rook, Pit, and Sorry! with our family, but I didn't mention it in class when we had lessons about keeping the Sabbath day holy, because I was afraid the teacher would think we weren't honoring the day properly.

As my Sabbath nitpicking progressed through seminary, institute, my mission, and into marriage, my list of "things you should never do on Sunday" was constantly being refined and expanded. When we began raising our children, I felt it was my responsibility to see that these cherished little ones learned and obeyed every aspect of these commandments too. Before long I had turned the Lord's Day of rest into our family's day of dread.

Getting ready for church was always a fiasco. Because of my husband's callings, he often had meetings or visits both before and after church. With children to dress, a baby to feed, and last-minute preparations for my own callings, I raced madly around in a determined frenzy. My aspirations for sweet and loving tones dissolved into angry yelling as I tried to hurry everyone along so we wouldn't be late. However, tardiness regularly prevailed just as it had in my childhood family.

The stress of getting *ready* for church was exceeded only by the stress of getting *through* church. It started as soon as I walked into the building and switched on my "happy face." I felt like a total hypocrite, but what other choice did I have? Everyone was watching! It was a critical moment for portraying the picture-perfect Molly Mormon family I so anxiously desired.

Sacrament meeting was an exercise in futility. No other family seemed to cause as much disturbance as we did. In my efforts to keep my little brood under control, I made quiet books, offered rewards, and inflicted punishments. Nothing I did seemed to have a positive effect for any length of time.

Though I wanted my children to be in church to learn about God, I was so entrenched in the fear of looking bad in other people's eyes that I didn't think about what my kids might be learning from *me*. As I reflect on those years, I can see that my unspoken message was often something like, "You really frustrate me when you don't act like perfect children at church." Sacrament meetings couldn't have been any more satisfying for them than they were for me.

When our church meetings were over for the day, the craziness didn't end. It was still the Sabbath, so there were still many rules to be enforced. No friends, no TV, no video games, no recreational cooking, no movies, no secular music, no breathing! Okay, maybe not that last one. But close.

My fearful, controlling approach created a vacuum. I knew what we *weren't* supposed to do, but the Sunday hours had to be filled with something, regardless of rules, and my kids were not going to sit around reading scriptures all day.

My Molly Mormon dream included a mother filling her family's Sunday hours with stories, games, and other carefully selected activities. I kept telling myself that I *had* to become that mother, but I usually did the essential food prep for my family and then dedicated the majority of the day to church callings and visiting widows. My children seemed happy to be left under the casual supervision of my husband, or as they got older, to manage themselves. In my absence, they filled the hours with whatever they could get away with. When I returned, I chastised them for their choices, but in my heart, I knew I was at fault for not being more organized and self-disciplined. It was my job to create a better balance in our home and make things work out the way they were supposed to.

Mother's Day was the worst Sunday of the year. My children showered me with hugs and homemade "I love you" cards, and they asked me to stay in my room so they could serve me breakfast in bed. My husband gave me fresh flowers and helped the kids in their efforts to make the day special for me. Speakers at church told stories of their incredible mothers who did all of the things I only wished I could do. Every well-intended effort to make me feel better made me feel more guilty and hypocritical because I *wasn't* a great mom. Though I longed to be the best mother imaginable—better than any mother in any story I had ever heard—I always saw myself failing miserably.

I don't want to leave the impression that nothing positive ever happened in our family. In spite of my need to control everything, there was a lot of love in our home, and we shared many good times together. However, the stumbling block that kept tripping me up was the constant fear that I wasn't living up to my precious Molly Mormon standard. I focused my attention on our shortcomings instead of rejoicing over our efforts and our progress. My family sensed my underlying feelings of disapproval, and that significantly diminished the amount of contentment we might have otherwise experienced.

One lovely activity I frequently involved my children with on Sundays was visiting widows and shut-ins. People always seemed to appreciate our visits, especially when we sang for them. Sister Larsen, one of our long-standing favorites, had a dog and fun toys to play with. I felt at peace during those visits, but as soon as we left, I was back to policing Sabbath behavior. Unfortunately our visits didn't take up the whole day, and my children became less interested in coming with me as they got older.

By the time our oldest children reached their early teens, almost every Sunday found us embroiled in conflict over something. Accumulating Church videos and a few other good movies that I proclaimed to be Sabbath-permissible brought some relief. We all have fond memories of Johnny Lingo and his eight-cow wife. The kids had the whole script to that movie memorized, but that didn't go far in resolving our Sabbath strife.

Eventually we began allowing friends to come over, as long as it was for a good purpose, like working on a Boy Scout merit badge or baking cookies for a Sunday School teacher. I worried that we were becoming too lax, but my husband was more on the kids' side than mine, so I knew I was losing the battle. Thankfully, God stepped in and ended the war.

Today I rejoice in the gift of the Sabbath day.

When God's amazing love changed my heart, I was free to embrace the spirit of the Sabbath and relinquish my smothering list of rules. Without the consuming fear of having my family shut out of the celestial kingdom, Sundays changed from my dreaded day to my favorite day. I began to treasure the Sabbath as a much-needed gift from a wise and loving Father who knows all too well how quickly this Molly Mortal can get distracted and lose sight of what is most important.

In God's great wisdom, He offers me one day in seven to pause and remember why I love His gospel so much. When I allow the Sabbath to fulfill its divine purpose, *the Lord's day of rest* becomes *my* day of rest—the rest I desperately need from the powerful enticings of the world. It can be a joyful time to renew my faith in God—my faith in His love, His mercy, and His eternal plan for His children.

By the time I experienced my change of heart, our children were old enough that getting ready for church was no longer a huge ordeal. They could all dress themselves and find something to eat if they needed a last minute snack before running out the door. And they could easily walk to church if they weren't ready when I was leaving.

Monte and I encouraged stragglers to be on time, but sometimes they didn't make it before the meeting started. Although there are many good reasons for being on time for church, the Spirit restrained me from making a big issue about their tardiness. I was quickly learning that the Lord is much more concerned about whether I treat my family with kindness than He is about arriving at church a few minutes late.

Sometimes the kids dozed off during sacrament meeting or chose to read a book they had brought along. If they weren't bothering anyone else, I didn't bother them, although I nudged them to listen if I heard something I thought they might particularly enjoy. Occasionally I tossed the old "settle down" look if they were hassling each other or otherwise creating a disturbance. But if I caught myself starting to worry about what people might be thinking, I quickly dismissed those thoughts. My church attendance was no longer about impressing others. My purpose was to fully participate in the meeting, involve myself with the Spirit, and enjoy worshipping with others, including my own family. Of course, I encouraged my children to listen and enjoy the meeting as much as they could, but honoring agency had begun to take its rightful place at the heart of my parenting.

Since I had happily retired from the burdensome job of Sabbath-day policing, I didn't spend a lot of time stressing about what my children chose to do after church. David didn't go to church anymore, so he usually slept late and then spent the rest of the day with friends. Periodically his behavior initiated conversations about agency with our other children, which ultimately seemed to help them solidify the way they felt about their own choices.

Occasionally we talked about what it really means to keep the Sabbath day holy and why certain activities might not be appropriate on Sunday. When given the opportunity to manage themselves, our children generally chose to honor the Sabbath. They sometimes played computer games or watched TV, but they also chose to attend church, watch Church videos, go to firesides with their friends, play board games together, and involve themselves in other good things. It was wonderful to enjoy the Sabbath with my family instead of battling constant frustration and guilt.

Interestingly enough, even with my change of heart, most of the things that fill my Sundays remain the same today. I go to church with my family, visit the elderly, and devote a significant amount of time to my callings. However, because my need to maintain the perfect Molly Mormon image no longer dominates my thinking, I'm much freer to receive and share God's love throughout the day. I'm also free to receive and enjoy the love of others instead of imagining what they might be thinking of me or my children.

Today when I think of the people I associate with on Sunday, I feel a wonderful sense of community. Of course, I don't always see eye to eye with everyone in my ward, but my heart is uniquely attached to my ward members. Rather than seeing them as harsh judges, I feel we somehow belong to one another. Maybe it's because we take care of each another in difficult times. We share our joys and our sorrows. Their commitment to the Savior strengthens me. We have a unique opportunity to build Zion together—a place where God's love abides unfettered, regardless of our human weaknesses.

The Doctrine and Covenants contains teachings regarding the Sabbath day that I have pondered and captured many times. I love how the Lord explains His purpose in having us meet together each Sunday: "And that thou *mayest more fully keep thyself unspotted from the world*, thou shalt go to the house of prayer and *offer up thy sacraments* upon my holy day; For verily this is a day appointed unto you to *rest from your labors* and to *pay thy devotions unto the Most High*."[2] The phrase, "that thou mayest more fully keep thyself unspotted from the world," really speaks to me. I've become convinced that meeting together, participating in the sacrament, and paying our devotions to God are central to His plan for defending us against worldly temptations.

One of my former Sunday rules was that you were supposed to attend all three hours of church regardless of anything else. It is still my intent to attend the full block of meetings each week, but without all of my old fears rattling around in my head, I'm open to other possibilities according to the Spirit's direction.

During sacrament meeting one day, I felt a repeated prompting to visit a certain sister. My initial thought was to wait until the end of the block, but because of a recurring sense of urgency,

I drove to her house instead of attending Sunday School. The minute I walked in the door I could feel the contention in her home and I knew I had been sent to help avert a serious conflict.

Today I feel a marvelous sense of freedom and peace in regard to the Sabbath. *This* day is not at all about following a rigid set of rules and regulations. It's about loving God and loving people. That's a joyful thought for a gregarious soul like me!

Though I often have quite a bit of discretionary time when Sunday rolls around, filling that time is never a problem. Generally, Monte and I try to read something together because we love sharing stories and ideas. Sometimes I read on my own, study gospel principles, or take a nap if I'm particularly tired. I love deciding which friends, family members, or new move-ins might enjoy a visit. Occasionally I have a definite sense of what the Lord would like me to share with someone, but often I go visiting simply because it feels like the right thing to do, and because it's so much fun. Sometimes my mother accompanies me. Other times we invite people to our home. The day always passes far too quickly.

True to my childhood tradition, I still like to prepare for the Sabbath on Saturday night by tidying up the house and mopping the kitchen floor. These physical preparations seem to help set the stage for a peaceful Sabbath the next day. However, if I need to take care of a housekeeping task on Sunday, I no longer have to deal with a mountain of guilt. One Sunday afternoon, I did a quick bathroom cleanup before company arrived because I realized I had overlooked that detail the night before. Years earlier, I would have cleaned more thoroughly to avoid being embarrassed, but I also would have been consumed with guilt for breaking the Sabbath. Thankfully that isn't my lot anymore.

When I do what I can to start the Sabbath with the Spirit, I find that I'm less likely to encounter a conflicting situation later in the day. However, if something arises that threatens to destroy the spirit of the Sabbath, I try to remember to turn to the Lord. When I do, I'm usually shown a way to be true to myself while allowing others to pursue their choices without any sense of judgment. Honoring agency is wonderfully freeing in countless situations!

Sometimes I hear people comment that calling Sunday "a day of rest" is a joke. I understand that sentiment completely. That is exactly how I felt for many years. It *is* a lot of work to get a family ready for church, wrestle children during meetings, fulfill demanding callings, and meet the other needs of the family throughout the day. Even without young children, Sundays can feel excessively busy rather than restful. When I had a stake calling that sometimes required me to attend two ward conferences on the same Sunday, I had precious little time for anything but meetings and getting ready for meetings.

On days like that, I remind myself that Sunday is my day to *set aside my own work and concentrate on doing God's work*, or as Isaiah puts it, the Sabbath is a day to "turn away [my] foot ... from doing [my own] pleasure."[3] Since experiencing my change of heart, I've discovered that even when my Sabbath work does make me physically tired, my Spirit is often joyfully refreshed and rejuvenated by the love I feel for God and for those I am serving.

And by the way, I found a clue for understanding the Lord's use of the word "rest." The scriptures say that entering into "his rest" is entering into "the fulness of his glory."[4] While taking a much-needed nap can indeed be "glorious," it is pretty obvious that observing the Lord's day of rest goes far beyond going to church and sleeping. Capturing that verse has yielded some lovely insights into the joy of the Sabbath on more than one occasion.

For the last several years, I have generally been able to sit peacefully through sacrament meeting, with my husband "doze meditating"* beside me. But sacrament meeting isn't always peaceful for me. I have eighteen lively grandchildren who visit us from time to time, giving me the opportunity to practice my changed-heart philosophy about children and church. Regardless of their ages, my goal is to help them have a pleasant *and* peaceful experience so they at least have a chance of feeling the Spirit.

My guiding principles are "Do everything from a place of love," and "Seek and follow the direction of the Spirit." My secret weapons are a peaceful attitude and a well-stocked church bag. Sometimes I've found it handy to have gum or small candies in my purse, though most often we do well without them.

Helping young children learn to happily respect the Sabbath can definitely be challenging. Approaching this goal from a place of peace rather than perfectionism has made an amazing difference for me. When we have children in our home on Sunday, we do fun activities with them like playing games, making cookies, reading stories, and going for a walk. We often watch a *Liken* movie[5] if there is time and interest. Perhaps my favorite Sunday activity is playing scripture charades. It opens the door to all kinds of family participation and creativity. It always takes much longer to get our skits ready than it does to

---

* Doze meditating is the term I came up with some time ago to describe my peaceful mental state when I lie in bed in the early morning with my mind drifting in and out of *meaningful* thought. Monte wants the same respectful term applied when he sits in church with his eyes closed and his head nodding. The jury is still out on that one!

reenact the scripture story, but that's not a problem because there is great fun in both.

Once I learned to establish a sense of connection with the Lord every day, the Sabbath became a special bonus day for me. Indeed it has become "a delight," to again use Isaiah's words.[6] The Sabbath is so much more than simply a day without chores. I feel a deep sense of gratitude to God for setting aside a specific time, and establishing a specific manner, for my spirit to be nurtured and rejuvenated each week.

Looking back on the various phases of my life, I realize that even during the years preceding my change of heart, church attendance, and fellowshipping with other members on the Sabbath, provided a critical anchor for me. Although I felt guilty, unworthy, and hopelessly inferior, for some reason I always felt drawn to be at church. My fears may have generally overpowered the whisperings of the Spirit, but regular attendance still provided me with a valuable routine during my floundering years of eating disorder and Molly Mormon perfectionism.

Yes, I occasionally still catch myself racing around on a Sunday morning, hoping I'll remember everything I need to do before I run out the door to church. And, no, I don't always remember to focus on the emblems of the sacrament during the meeting as much as I intend to. That's why I have the sacrament prayers taped in the front of my scriptures. If I realize that my mind has inexplicably wandered when I meant for it to stay focused, I flip open the cover and tenderly review those precious words.

This Molly Mortal, in all her weakness, really does want to always have His Spirit to be with her. But God knows that at any moment my nearsighted human nature may easily distract me from what I want most. He mercifully offers me a weekly space, along with simple religious rituals, to help me set the world aside and focus my eyes and my heart on the needs of my eternal spirit.

President McKay says, "If we seek [God] on the Sabbath day [and] get into his presence on that day, we shall find it less difficult to be in his presence the following days of the week."[7] Being in His presence so that I can confidently live in His peace, love, and joy is the real gift I am seeking. The Sabbath day helps me transform that possibility into a reality.

5

LET THE HUNGER PAINS BEGIN

Finding Joy in Observing the Fast God Has Chosen

I confess that fasting mostly meant just going hungry.

Turning eight years old was an exciting time for me, because I had been taught that when I got baptized, all my sins would be washed away. Between those note-taking angels we sang about, and my propensity for naughtiness, there was a lot of bad stuff that needed to be washed off my heavenly slate.

There was, however, one huge drawback about turning eight, and that was fasting. In our family, when you got baptized you had to start skipping breakfast on fast Sundays. I hated feeling hungry, and having my mother tell me that some children went to bed hungry every night didn't help at all.

My parents tried to ease us into fasting gradually. At eight, we were only required to fast one meal, but once we turned twelve it was the whole deal—twenty-four hours and not a minute less—or sundown to sundown, whichever you preferred. Either way, it meant that I was in for what seemed like an eternity of a grumbling stomach. Giving in to the temptation to sneak a piece of bread was not an option. Those note-taking angels were busy writing everything down, so God would immediately know I was being naughty again.

At some point I was taught that if I decided on a *purpose* for my fast and then prayed about it while I wasn't eating, God would be more likely to do what I wanted Him to. I'd already decided He wasn't eager to answer my prayers, but this made it sound like fasting with a purpose was a way to twist God's arm a little. As long as I had to suffer through the hunger pains anyway, I might as well do all I could to get something good out of it.

I couldn't always figure out what purpose I should assign to my fasts, but our bishop or stake president sometimes asked us to fast for rain or snow to avert impending crop failure. During a particularly severe drought, the stake president asked us to fast both Saturday *and* Sunday—forty-eight long hours! I was glad my parents didn't require me to fast the whole time, but when I went to Sunday School that week, I wished I had. Some of my classmates quizzed everyone to determine who had held out the longest, and I felt bad that I wasn't the winner.

I remember having letter-of-the-law discussions at home and at church about what the Lord might consider a "true" fast. We agreed you were supposed to start and end your fast with prayer, but did it have to be a personal prayer? Could the closing prayer at church count for ending your fast if your twenty-four hours were up? Could you chew gum while you were fasting? Could you have a tiny sip of water if your mouth was really dry? What if you swished the water around in your mouth and then spit it out? Did God count it at all if you didn't fast the whole day? Could you eat a treat that your teacher gave you, or did you have to wait until you got home so you could end your fast with a prayer? What if you went into an empty classroom after church and said a quick prayer to end your fast? *Then* could you eat your treat?

Not surprisingly, my family almost always came down on the side of greatest restriction, so when I saw someone chewing gum or stopping at the drinking fountain on fast Sunday, I was sure they weren't being righteous. On the way home from church we would condemn the teachers who had handed out treats, because it tempted class members to break their fast before they were supposed to. I'm sure my parents and teachers tried to help me understand the spirit of the fast rather than just the rules, but my young mind wasn't yet able to get beyond the dos and don'ts, much less my hunger.

From time to time I heard amazing stories about the results of people's fasting—people at death's door were miraculously healed; antagonistic family members' hearts were softened, and they were baptized. Sometimes the stories were so touching that I wept, but I could never see any fruits of my own fasting. As with other situations, I often felt secretly jealous, and assumed that those blessings were reserved for people who were more spiritual than I was. Still, I kept fasting each month, partly because that is what we did in our family, and partly because I didn't want God to be mad at me.

During my late teens and early twenties, my eating disorder entangled itself with the concept of fasting. After an especially intense period of bingeing and purging, I often "fasted" for as many days as I possibly could, hoping to show God that I was finally deserving of His intervention. Ignoring my hunger pains gave me a temporary sense of power over my compulsion to binge and purge. Maybe that was a sign that God was ready to help me manage my bizarre life.

The sense of control felt like a spiritual high, but those "fasts" were clearly not based on true principles. In the end, they made me more miserable, because as soon as I got too hungry to "fast" anymore, I inevitably reverted to my pattern of bingeing and purging. Then I would viciously attack myself for losing control *again*, and for foolishly thinking that God might want to help me when I was so pathetic and weak.

After I married and the eating disorder no longer plagued my life, I didn't fast for fifteen months because I was pregnant and then nursing. When I did fast again, going without food for twenty-four hours was not a big deal. I'd had a lot of practice starving myself for much longer than that. However, all of my Molly Mormon rules about fasting stepped up to make sure I was doing it "right." I tried to remember to start my fast immediately after lunch on Saturday so we could eat as soon as we got home from church the next day.

Once I'd said the prayer to start my fast, I was vigilant because my rules declared me a fast-breaker if I forgot and swallowed a tiny bit of water while brushing my teeth. When I broke a rule, I had to start the twenty-four hours over again if I wanted to please God. It irritated me when people scheduled wedding receptions or other activities on the evening before fast Sunday. I hated being forced to choose between fancy refreshments and keeping my fast on schedule. Sometimes, though, I felt quite self-righteous for observing the fast in the face of desserts that seemed almost irresistible.

When it came to teaching my own children about fasting, I felt a lot of conflict. They didn't like hunger pains any more than I had as a kid, but I wanted to help them practice this gospel principle "correctly." As always, my motive had everything to do with getting us all to the celestial kingdom. More immediately,

I didn't want their Primary teachers to think I was a bad mother for not training them properly, and I didn't want my children to be embarrassed when the Primary president asked everyone who was fasting to raise their hands.

At first I tried to implement the same guidelines I had been raised with—skip one meal after you're baptized, then skip two when you turn twelve. My husband agreed that our children should be taught to fast, but the job of policing the kitchen naturally fell to me. Though our kids *wanted* to be good, they also had those relentless hunger pains gnawing at their stomachs. Monte and I talked with them about fasting with a purpose and often decided who or what we wanted to fast for as a family, but that did little to curb their complaining.

When our older children reached their teen years, and the conflict increased, my husband encouraged me to surrender to agency so I could have some peace. He reasoned that we had taught them a correct principle and now I needed to let them govern themselves. Consequently we decided that on the Saturday before fast Sunday I would post a big reminder note in the kitchen that said, "Fast Sunday tomorrow." The next morning I would make no effort to patrol the fridge or pantry, and I would refrain from asking the kids if they were fasting.

As soon as I implemented this new plan, the fast Sunday attitude in our home improved. Though I definitely had my reservations, I usually only heard grumbling on Saturday when they first noticed the sign. Most of the time, they each chose to fast for at least part of Sunday. But my Molly Mormon fears were still firmly in place, and I worried that I was failing to help them be good enough for God.

Today I rejoice in fasting as a pathway to freedom and oneness with God.

Because I hadn't been monitoring my children's fasting when I experienced my change of heart, I didn't notice as much of a difference in our home regarding this principle as I did with Sabbath-day observance. I did, however, begin to give myself more leeway about how long I fasted. I generally followed the guideline of skipping two meals, but choosing when to break my fast was not so much about the clock as it was about how I was feeling physically and spiritually. The timing also varied depending on what the demands of my day happened to be. I relaxed about having to pray right when I started my fast, although I still liked to have a specific purpose for my fast which I mentioned in my prayers. Ending my fast with a prayer always seemed to help me feel grateful and more connected to God.

Releasing the guilt and frustration around fasting allowed new blessings to come into my life. I could rejoice with others in their success stories about fasting instead of feeling jealous. When I sensed I was falling into the habit of eating too much junk food during the month, I welcomed fast day as a new beginning for creating a needed change. When I fasted with others for a predetermined purpose, I enjoyed the feeling of uniting our hearts in a common desire.

But truly *rejoicing* in the blessing of the fast finally came when I decided to make fasting the focus of my scripture study. When I first used LDS View to search for the word "fasting," I had no idea what an amazing journey I had initiated. One verse immediately caught my attention. It said, "And on this day [the Sabbath] thou shalt do none other thing, only let thy food be prepared with singleness of heart that thy fasting may be perfect, or, in other words, that thy joy may be full. Verily, this is fasting and prayer, or in other words, rejoicing and prayer."[1] Hmmm, two of my favorite words in the same verse—joy and rejoicing—in a verse talking about *fasting*! That was a pretty obvious clue that there was much more to fasting than just going hungry.

As I began working through other scripture references, I soon found a wonderful treasure tucked away near the end of that daunting book of Isaiah. Capturing the fifty-eighth chapter proved to be a most enlightening experience for me. In the first few verses, I learned that the Israelites had been fasting and afflicting themselves with sackcloth and ashes, and yet God was not responding to their cries. That sounded familiar, though of course, I hadn't literally done the sackcloth-and-ashes thing.

In the next verses, the Lord explains that his lack of response to their cries is because of their contentious practices, but then He changes the focus by asking a question: "Is not this the fast that I have chosen?"

Then the Lord explains that the purpose of fasting is "to loose the bands of wickedness, to undo the heavy burdens, to let the oppressed go free, and that ye break every yoke."[2] My heart truly rejoiced as I considered those words. Wow! Fasting is really all about freedom!

My immediate thought was about how fasting could free *me* from spiritual bondage, but I soon realized that by fasting in the Lord's way, I could free both myself *and* others from bondage. Awesome—two for the price of one!

The next verses list things I can include in my fasting to create an increase of freedom, like caring for the poor and making myself available to my family. But then, even before the Lord finishes explaining how He wants me to observe the fast, He starts listing an abundance of amazing blessings that He is anxious to pour out upon those who fast His way—things like health and light and protection. As I continued capturing these verses, my heart swelled with love for the Savior, and I felt an overwhelming surge of gratitude and joy.

Because of my change of heart experience, I understood what He was talking about in verse nine when he said, "Then shalt thou call, and the Lord shall answer; thou shalt cry, and he shall say, Here I am." His tender response to my desperate cry that day had blessed my life beyond anything I had ever imagined.

Later in verse nine, God adds another aspect of fasting that also caused me to pause and ponder. He says to "take away from the midst of thee the yoke, the putting forth of the finger, and speaking vanity." In the NIV Bible,[3] that verse is translated as "the pointing finger and malicious talk." As I thought about this aspect of God's chosen fast, the Spirit whispered to me that this was the "yoke" that had plagued my life and held my heart hostage for so many years. God had wanted to free me of that heavy burden long before I was ready to leave it at his feet.

Isaiah concludes his message on fasting with several amazing promises expressed in beautiful "Isaiah-ese"—promises about becoming a light, a nurturer, a healer, a spring of unfailing water. By the end of the chapter, I could clearly see that the Lord's chosen fast is designed to bring my heart into oneness with His. He is offering this Molly Mortal a way to become joyfully free by laying her natural-woman tendencies on His altar and by joining Him in His work. The way I counted, God asks me to include seven things in my fasting, and in return, He promises sixteen amazing blessings. Not a bad return on my investment!

Is it any wonder that as each fast Sunday rolls around, I open my scriptures and focus on God's chosen fast according to Isaiah? It's a fabulous reminder of the reasons I skip two perfectly good meals each month and put up with a few hunger pains. As I review these few verses and write new thoughts that come to mind, I do my best to discern what the Lord would like me to do *that very day*, rather than relying on a long list of stringent rules to govern my fast. No matter how many times I return to this chapter, I'm always blessed with tender feelings and inspiration.

Isaiah has wondrously broadened my understanding. Fasting now seems to be much more about keeping my baptismal covenants—or, you might say, "about practicing godliness"—than about abstaining from food. It's a way for me to share in Christ's mission of binding up the brokenhearted, liberating the captive, and comforting those who mourn.[4] It's a tool that helps me do the things I need to be mindful of all the time if I want to enjoy the companionship of the Lord.

The traditional fast I was taught in my youth—abstaining from food, offering prayers that focus on the purpose of my fast, and paying fast offerings—can be a great spiritual practice. Going without food for a period of time serves as an excellent reminder of my dependence on the Lord's sustaining power and grace. Praying for the purpose of my fast can draw me closer to the Lord when I take the time to truly connect with Him. Making a financial contribution to ease the physical burdens of an unknown recipient is a very good thing to do. But my rejoicing increases immensely when I review the Lord's fast in Isaiah's terms and then create an experience based on the guidance I receive for my fast that particular day.

Sweet blessings have come as I've fasted in this manner. On occasion I've followed promptings to visit specific sisters and discovered that each one urgently needed some kind of assistance. Other times I have found that they just needed to see a friendly face or talk about a challenge they were facing.

One day I felt I should send a young mother a specific amount of money. When she received it, she called and told me she had been praying about the needs of her four-year-old daughter. She felt she should enroll her in a certain program, but their family budget didn't have the flexibility to pay for it. She had a little money tucked away, and when she combined it with what I had sent her, she was able to cover the fee.

On another fast Sunday when I asked the Lord how He wanted me to observe the fast, I felt I should take some money to a young woman who was preparing for a mission. I usually give new missionaries a check on the day they give their departing talks in sacrament meeting, but she wasn't scheduled to speak for another month. However, I gladly followed the prompting and left an envelope at her door. Later I learned that she had been stressed because she had run out of money and still needed to buy a heavy winter coat since she was going to serve in a very cold area. The amount I gave her was exactly what she needed to buy the coat she'd already picked out.

There have been times when, for health reasons, I've felt I shouldn't abstain from food on a particular fast Sunday. There have also been times when I've considered petitioning the Lord for a certain blessing by fasting frequently or for an extended period of time. In some of these instances, the Spirit has whispered to me that such a fast would be unwise, but He's also reminded me that I can gain the benefits of the fast by purifying my heart, lifting the hearts of others, and attending to the needs of those around me.

Abstaining from a specific food, such as sugar, soda, or chocolate for an extended period has also proven to be a very meaningful "fast" for me, especially when I remember to combine it with sincere prayer. Such was the case when we sent out our first missionary.

Since our oldest son hadn't gone on a mission, I was particularly excited to have our second son accept his call. I enthusiastically helped him prepare for his departure, but on the day he entered the MTC, a dark, almost tangible cloud overshadowed me. I kept thinking it would soon leave, but I absolutely could not shake it, and weeks later, it still hung heavily over me.

Finally, I took my scriptures outside on my deck, opened them to the missionary sections in the early part of the Doctrine and Covenants, and had an intense talk with God. I told Him I couldn't see how I could possibly live under that bleak cloud for two whole years, and I begged Him for the peace and comfort He promises to those who earnestly seek Him. To my great relief, He immediately lifted the darkness from my heart.

Shortly thereafter, I was impressed to abstain from eating chocolate while my son was on his mission. Not only was I directed not to eat chocolate, but each time I had the opportunity to refuse it, I was to turn my thoughts to the Lord and offer a silent prayer for my missionary. (I was amazed by the number of prayers I ended up saying in a single day!) The peace and comfort I received from the Lord in regards to our missionary was so remarkable that when our next son left for his mission a few years later, I began a similar fast for him.

I've found that fasting from an undesirable habit like procrastinating, criticizing, or staying up too late is another way of inviting an increase of the Spirit into my life. As I combine this kind of fasting with earnest prayer and scripture study, I feel the Lord's strengthening influence freeing me to choose a better way.

When my husband was a BYU bishop, he challenged the ward to do a twenty-four-hour fast, not from food, but from all faultfinding—that putting forth of the finger that Isaiah talked about. Monte asked the ward to start over if they slipped up so that they could experience a full day without finding fault with anyone. Most ward members were shocked to realize how frequently critical thoughts came to their minds. A few students said they were left totally speechless. Hardly anyone was able to complete a full "twenty-four-hour faultfinding fast" that week, but we all agreed that the attempt had blessed our lives.

Another time, my husband challenged our children to fast from complaining for a full day. Their efforts to observe that fast helped them realize how much they had been complaining, and it was also a pleasant gift to me. This kind of fasting seems very much in keeping with the counsel of Isaiah, and must surely evoke many of the blessings promised to those who fast.

Today when I seek to make a fast particularly effective, I'm now aware of many options that can enhance my efforts. My new perspective on fasting has brought me both joy and a measure of spiritual confidence. I'll probably never know exactly how much my fasting influences God's willingness to grant specific blessings I seek, but this much I do know: fasting in the Lord's way brings me closer to being one with Him.

Fasting also helps me overcome my natural woman tendencies so I can think and act in a more Christlike way. It has the power to open my heart and make me more sensitive to the revelations and promptings of the Holy Ghost. It softens my heart and leads me to not only *feel* compassion for others, but also to *do what I can* to ease their burdens. When I open my scriptures to that well-worn page of Isaiah and ask God how He would like me to observe the fast for that particular day, I often feel like I am embarking on an exciting adventure.

Before I came to know God's loving nature, I measured the success of my fasts by how many rules I followed perfectly. I stressed and strained over which rules were most important and wondered if God ever took my determined efforts into consideration. Thank goodness that is all behind me. Now I gratefully rejoice in the knowledge that the law of the fast is a gift of God that yields humility and helps me draw closer to Him. Fasting offers me another wonderful avenue for approaching a fullness of His joy.

6

EVEN MY HOSANNA SHOUT WASN'T GOOD ENOUGH

Discovering the Treasures of Temple Worship

I confess that I found the temple confusing and boring.

During my childhood, the nearest temple was about eighty miles from our home, so regular temple attendance represented a significant sacrifice for my parents. Not only did it stress their limited budget, but it also meant they would be spending a whole day away from home. It was no simple task to arrange everything so they could be gone from their young family, their thirsty crops, and their demanding livestock. Nevertheless, they were diligent in their efforts to go to the temple every month.

I remember sitting on my parents' bed when I was about ten or eleven, watching my mother iron temple clothes in preparation for their trip the next day. She told me she had sewn the clothing herself and paused to show me her beautiful handwork. As she carefully pressed the long rows of white pleats, I began asking questions. How was the clothing worn? What did people actually *do* in the temple besides get married?

Mother said that when you went to the temple, you made sacred covenants, but you weren't supposed to talk about them outside of the temple, so she couldn't tell me very much. Although she was comfortable showing me the clothing, she explained that it wasn't appropriate for her to put it on outside of the temple. This sparked more questions, but I was again told that I would have to wait for answers until I was old enough to go through the temple myself.

As I lay in bed that night reflecting on our conversation, more questions arose. Why did things about the temple have to be such a big secret? What mysteries were hidden there that I couldn't know until I was older?

Long before that experience, I decided that I was going to be married in the temple. From my earliest years, I remember Mother saying that being married to Daddy in the temple was her most precious blessing. The importance of temple marriage was repeatedly taught in Sunday School, Primary, and Young Women lessons, as well as being preached over the pulpit. It sounded as if being married in the temple was the only way to have a happy life, and the only kind of marriage acceptable to God.

Throughout my youth, I dreamed of someday going to the temple with a worthy, amazing, thoughtful, good-looking, young priesthood holder, and being sealed together forever. On August 16, 1972, that dream came true. Monte and I made our wedding vows across an altar in the Idaho Falls Temple, stepping into the long-awaited future of eternal marriage. Like my mother, I deeply cherish that event.

Although I had a minimal understanding of temple covenants at the time, I believed that the temple is the house of God and that the ordinances performed there were essential to achieving my goal of Molly Mormon happiness. However, during the next almost thirty years, my true feelings about the temple would probably have best been described as guilty, confused, and frustrated. I didn't go often enough, I didn't love being there, and I didn't have a clear understanding of what I was being taught when I did go. Other church members seemed to have all kinds of spiritual experiences as a result of their temple attendance. Many said the temple was their favorite place on earth. That certainly wasn't the case for me.

Of course, the temple was peaceful and quiet, but the ordinances felt redundant and impossible to understand. The mystery surrounding temple work had not gone away. I wanted to be among those who talked about the strength they received from temple attendance or who said they learned something new each time they went. Instead, I usually left feeling spiritually defective because I just didn't get it.

My husband's feelings about the temple were the exact opposite of mine. He loved studying temple-related topics in the scriptures and delighted in each new insight he gained.

When I first took him home to meet my parents, they picked us up from the bus station in Idaho Falls, and we went to the temple together. Two things about Monte totally won my mother's heart that day. Not only was he comfortable and playful with her, but at the end of our temple session, he responded to the call for volunteers—a request often made at the time, when extra men were needed for the final ordinance work. She had never seen anyone so young step forward, and she was impressed by his confidence.

During the months of our courtship, there was a lot of excitement in Utah Valley over the construction of the Provo Temple. Temple attendance would soon be much easier, not only for local members, but also for BYU students and missionaries in the Language Training Mission (later called the Missionary Training Center).

A few months prior to our engagement, Monte and I went to the Marriott Center for one of the temple dedication services. President Harold B. Lee, then a counselor in the First Presidency, led the Hosanna Shout. Right in the middle of it, he stopped and sternly reprimanded the congregation for our lack of enthusiasm. Most of us were BYU students with little temple experience, and I resented his chastisement. Of course I felt guilty for those feelings, but his criticism really bothered me and left another troubling shadow in the corner of my mind.

After the dedication, Monte and I attended the Provo Temple several times. It was exciting to be there together as we anticipated our upcoming wedding, but I didn't know how to appreciate his enthusiasm about temple ordinances and symbolism. It was embarrassing when I couldn't remember specific details like he did, or some exact wording that had caught his attention. I was afraid he'd think he was marrying a spiritual loser.

Once we were married, I usually enjoyed going to the temple, as long as we invited another couple to go along with us. I was glad for the social interaction while appeasing Molly Mormon's nagging reprimand that I should be there more often. After the session, we often ate in the temple cafeteria so we could freely discuss temple-related topics. Rarely did I contribute to those conversations, but I liked watching Monte impress our friends with his knowledge and insights.

Though I wished I could be more of a temple scholar, what I really wanted was the self-improvement that Church leaders promised to those who faithfully went to the temple. After I began parenting, my character flaws seemed to be magnified a hundredfold, particularly my lack of patience. It was clear that if we were ever going to match my ideal Molly Mormon family, I had to become a much better person.

Thus, the temple was the center of a great dilemma for me: I really wanted the blessings promised for regular attendance, but I didn't really want to go.

Opportunities constantly appeared to pile on the guilt. Talks in church focused on the blessings of temple attendance and emphasized the shame we should feel if we failed to go regularly. After all, we had several temples within a few hours' drive. Thus, whenever I *did* make it to the temple, it was usually because I was ashamed of myself, not because I had any desire to be there. I had heard that doing the right thing for the wrong reason was better than not doing it at all, and I sincerely hoped God felt that way about my temple attendance.

Eventually I devised a plan for consistent weekly attendance. Every Tuesday morning, I got up at 4:30 a.m., hurried to catch the first session of the day, then raced back home to take over the care of our two little boys so Monte could get to work or school on time. I hoped to prove to God that I was worthy of being changed into the perfect spiritual person I longed to be.

Unfortunately, keeping that early schedule didn't change me into a spiritual powerhouse. Instead, it changed me into a tired, even-more-stressed, even-less-patient mother. Ultimately my exhaustion increased much more than my spirituality, so after several months, I gave up on my early morning temple jaunts.

Through the years, Monte and I attended ward temple nights. It was a pleasant way to maintain the image of a righteous Church member and at the same time soothe my guilt. After our children were all in school, I began attending the temple each month with other Relief Society sisters. We called this activity TLC: temple, lunch, and conversation. I still think that's a clever spin-off from the original meaning of "tender loving care."

For TLC, sisters would gather at the church, carpool to the temple, attend an endowment session, and then have lunch together. Again, I couldn't say I enjoyed the temple experience itself, but I enjoyed socializing and the momentary relief from guilt, since I was doing what I was "supposed" to. Unfortunately, "doing the right thing" did not noticeably change my attitude about the redundancy of the ordinances. Nor did it reduce the frustration and confusion I felt about temple worship.

In spite of my own hang-ups, I wanted our children to view the temple as a sacred place, a special place they would someday be allowed to enter. After each child's baptism, we drove to the Provo Temple and walked to the east side, where it says, "The House of the Lord. Holiness to the Lord." I hoped this tradition would encourage them to live according to God's commandments so they would be ready for their own temple covenants at the appropriate time. Secretly, though, I worried that I was being hypocritical, because I lacked the desire to be in the temple myself.

Throughout my life, I often heard older parents say they were deeply grateful that all of their children had married in the temple. It seemed to me like they were bragging more than actually feeling grateful, and I worried about how people felt whose children *hadn't* all married in the temple. Nevertheless, as my children grew, I found myself anxiously aspiring to that same goal. I wanted my children's families to be safely sealed to my forever family, and having each of them marry in the temple was an important step on the path.

One of the most despairing moments of my life came not long after David told me he was gay. For some reason, a thought popped into my mind, seemingly out of nowhere, and clearly stated, "You're never going to be happy. All of your children will never be married in the temple."

I spiraled into a black hole as the words repeated in my mind.

I'm never going to be happy. I'm never going to be happy! I'M NEVER GOING TO BE HAPPY! My knowledge of the temple ordinances seemed to be condemning me to endless misery instead of bringing me eternal happiness.

Today I rejoice in the sweet influence the temple brings to my life.

When my love for God replaced my Molly Mormon obsession, my attitude toward temple attendance softened. I can't say that I immediately gained an appreciation for the temple ordinances, or that I felt any particular eagerness to attend. However, I did notice that the disquieting feelings were gone. Ward temple nights and TLC activities still seemed more of a social opportunity than a time to draw near to the Lord, but at least the guilt no longer plagued me.

Years passed before I came across a recording by S. Michael Wilcox entitled "That All Their Outgoings from This House May Be in the Name of the Lord."[1] Brother Wilcox quoted Isaiah to point out how the Lord pleads with us to come to His temples, feast at His table, and take shelter from the storms of life. As I listened to his words, the Spirit carried them deep into my heart and quickened my understanding.

For some reason, it suddenly dawned on me that the same tender, merciful God who had rescued me from my darkest hour and filled my life with love and light was the same God who had put all of the symbolism and redundancy into the temple. He was the same loving God I rejoiced in during my morning prayers and scripture study, the same God who anchored me during my times of stress or crisis. Listening to this talk helped me realize that the temple ordinances and their symbolism are an incredible manifestation of God's perfect love for His children.

Before concluding his talk, Brother Wilcox referred to a wondrous temple vision shown to Ezekiel by a heavenly messenger. In that vision, Ezekiel saw an ever-increasing river of water that flowed from the temple, bringing life to the barren land.[2] Perhaps because of my childhood experiences during drought years, Brother Wilcox's description of that abundant, flowing water mesmerized me. I eagerly searched out the reference and studied the vision in Ezekiel's own words. Reading those verses filled my heart with an urge to race to the temple, figuratively throw my arms around the Savior, and bask in the delight of my new understanding. My temple attendance immediately became a happily anticipated, regular event.

No longer did I feel that I should somehow be concocting a notable spiritual experience every time I went. I simply rejoiced in the feelings that drew my heart to His house. Each time I approached the temple doors, I looked over at the fountain and recalled Ezekiel's vision of Christ's living water pouring forth to heal the land. That living water was gently healing another aspect of my life.

In addition to the original fountain, a beautiful reflection pool has been added near the entrance of the Provo Temple. Whenever I'm leaving the temple, I usually take the few extra steps required to pass by the pool and lightly run my fingers through the water as it slips over the edge. This little ritual has become an act of worship and devotion for me—a way of expressing my gratitude to God for His living water which endlessly flows into my life.

Brother Wilcox's talk was just the beginning. Since then I've become aware of the abundance of temple references in the scriptures, and I've noticed many similarities between temple language and scripture language. I savor the questions and insights that come as I study about the temple. I've been led to scripture passages, books and firesides that have continued to increase my understanding. Monte's research for his calling as a gospel doctrine teacher has been a great instigator of temple discussions in Sunday School, as well as in our home.

One insight that probably would have been obvious to me from the beginning, if I hadn't been so caught up in my Molly Mormon fears, is that temple worship shows the pattern for entering God's presence. The thing I treasure the most is feeling His presence in my life. God wants me to enter His presence. In the temple, I'm shown the way to actually do that.

Today I feel peace and contentment as I attend the temple. Sometimes I go with a question regarding symbols or doctrine. Sometimes I go with a simple desire to express my love and appreciation to God and to rejoice in the opportunity of being in His house. Sometimes I'm able to perform vicarious ordinances for my ancestors. Other times I go seeking guidance or special blessings for myself, for family members, or for dear friends.

Regardless of my purpose for being in the temple, I always try to consciously open my heart to God's love and inspiration. Those efforts have been generously rewarded, not only with insights about the temple, but also with ideas for my writing, inspiration for healing troubled relationships, and a feeling of optimism about life.

After it finally clicked that the God I know and love so dearly in my personal life is anxiously awaiting me in His holy house, all of my temple concerns resolved themselves in one way or another. The repetition of the temple ceremony now makes perfect sense when I consider that each time I attend, I'm making covenants for deceased women, and that the temple experience is new *for them.* I remind myself that I'm a guest listening in on their covenants, and that as I do so, I'm allowed the privilege of reviewing my own covenants.

Although I hear the same words each time, it is similar to studying my favorite passages from the scriptures. New thoughts, questions, and inspiration continue to arise. Even when I struggle to stay alert and attentive, I feel grateful for the redundancy rather than resistant to it. I want to be in the temple often so I can continue to learn and build on the knowledge God has already given me.

Understanding temple symbolism has become an ongoing quest. Since symbolism is God's way of hiding things in plain sight, I pray for eyes to see and for greater ability to understand what He is offering me. Sometimes I'm blessed with a real "aha moment," but most often I leave with a few simple thoughts to ponder, along with a sweet feeling of gratitude. I no longer stress that I can't see more in this moment, even though I know I'm only catching a fraction of what is available.

Now that I can freely enjoy my own exploration of temple symbolism, the sense of mystery which began all those years ago has been replaced with a sense of gratitude for each little bit of increased understanding. Nothing excites my soul like the anticipation of Christ's loving embrace, and being welcomed into the presence of our Heavenly Father. The temple allows me to experience that moment symbolically each time I do an endowment session.

Temple symbolism has become a joy to me, whether I'm reviewing simple ideas I have known for years, or pondering truths I'm just beginning to discover. As I put on fresh garments each morning, I symbolically dedicate my physical and spiritual strength to God and receive His protective shield over my life. Somehow this daily routine makes me feel connected to faithful women in the Bible who also looked to the temple as a place of strength and refuge.

When I change into my white temple dress, I reflect on my desire to put off the natural woman and become more like Christ through His merciful Atonement. Seeing everyone dressed in white reminds me that we are all equal before God, and that His blessings are available to every soul who comes to Him in faith and follows His Son's example. Putting on temple robes helps me ponder the beautiful, eternal blessings God is eager for me to receive.

While I still enjoy attending the temple with my husband and with friends, I find my attendance particularly rewarding when I go by myself. Going alone allows me to focus more completely on my thoughts, on my questions, and on the impressions that come to my heart. Even though we go through the endowment as a group, I often feel a very personal connection with God. Sometimes I visualize myself kneeling before the Savior at the altar and laying my burdens before Him. I ask for His comforting, healing touch, as well as for the strength and wisdom to deal with them in His way.

Another concern that God has resolved for me is regarding my "forever family." When I feared that one of my precious children might never marry in the temple, and therefore not "make it" to the celestial kingdom, I lived in turmoil. Experiencing God's love freed me to trust life, to trust God, and to realize that each member of my family is in His hands. The Spirit has whispered this comforting truth to me over and over as I have opened my heart to Him. *All* things are in His hands, and I can trust Him.

The Lord has promised us that as we attend the temple, our families *will* be blessed. Having faith in Him means that I'm willing to let Him be in charge of what those blessings look like.

In resolving my temple concerns, God has even given me a gentle antidote to my negative feelings toward President Lee. With the construction of new temples in Utah, members in surrounding communities have been invited to participate in the dedicatory services as they have been broadcast into our stake centers. I have taken every opportunity to attend those meetings, and I'm grateful that President Lee taught me to enthusiastically join with the hosts of heaven in the joyous moment of the Hosanna Shout. I'm grateful for my current understanding that the restoration of temple ordinances is truly something to shout about!

Today I'm thankful to be among those who live close to many temples, but I'm even more grateful that an abundance of joy surrounds my temple attendance. I admit that there are still occasions when going to the temple ends up feeling more routine than spiritual or joyful. Perhaps I'll never be among those who say they learn something new every time they go, but the sense of mystery and frustration has been replaced with a sense of gratitude and adoration. As I approach the temple doors, I try to remember to pause, look up at the spire, and visualize myself stepping into another world, a world filled with God's presence—His truth, His light, and His perfect love.

While looking up, I like to think of the words Christ spoke to the Brother of Jared when he asked the Lord not to confuse their language, and to guide them to a new land. On that occasion, Christ told him to gather his family, his friends, and their flocks, and go to a valley northward. Then He said, "And there will I meet thee."[3] Something wonderful happens in my heart as I pause to visualize Christ waiting to meet me on the other side of the temple doors, eager to lead me to the spiritual feast He has set before His children in His holy house.

It recently occurred to me that when I turn my heart to God in my home and feel His presence with me, He is essentially accepting my invitation to visit me in *my* house. On the other hand, when I take the time to go to the temple, I'm physically accepting His invitation to visit Him in *His* house. His open invitation reminds me that He truly wants me to feast at His table and receive spiritual nourishment there. He wants me to savor each bite and take home with me the spiritual strength I gain.[4]

Though this Molly Mortal is not yet prepared or able to receive all that has been spread before her, I sense that God is pleased with my desire and efforts to come often and partake in whatever way I can.

7

NEIGHBORS— WHO NEEDS THEM?

Joyfully Sharing God's Love

I confess that the commandment to love your neighbor seemed impossible.

When I was very young, I didn't think that the commandment to love your neighbor applied to me. I thought only people who lived right next door to someone else had neighbors, and we lived in the country. The closest house to ours was almost half a mile away. No neighbors, no worries!

But then someone explained that "neighbor" meant anyone you associated with, not just those who happened to live nearby. This bit of information was most unwelcome. It sent my young mind reeling into an abyss of confusion and guilt, because now I was supposed to love a whole bunch of people I didn't even like.

Of course I liked the people who were really nice to me, but I would never have said I *loved* them. And there was nothing to love, or even like, about some of our nearest neighbors. They were downright scary. They cussed and smoked and drank, and their kids were always causing trouble on the school bus. A few of the older kids would sneak down our lane at night and steal gas from my dad's big fuel tank. How was I supposed to love people like that? Anything resembling good feelings, much less *love*, seemed out of the question.

Sometime later, my Sunday School teacher related the story of the Good Samaritan and told us that every person in the world was a "neighbor." I was dumbfounded. It was absolutely mind-boggling to consider that God expected me to follow such a commandment. No way could I ever love so many strange, unknown people, even if I wanted to—which I definitely did not!

Trying to wrap my mind around the concept of love was so confusing. A significant part of my early perceptions came from the romantic old reel-to-reel movies we watched every Friday night at the church house. They portrayed true love as an overpowering attraction between a beautiful girl and a handsome guy. It caused them to fall in love and then persist in spite of whatever challenges, until they arrived at the blissful threshold of happily ever after.

It didn't seem possible that such romantic beginnings could be the forerunners of the marriages I was familiar with. Though I was fortunate to have parents who were affectionate with each other, they didn't seem nearly as passionate about their love as the people I saw on the big screen. And most of the other couples I observed didn't appear to have nearly as pleasant a relationship as my parents did. Mother assured me that she and Daddy shared a much deeper love than my favorite movie couples did, but I wasn't yet mature enough to comprehend what she was trying to tell me.

In our community, most husbands worked long, hard hours to provide for their families, and most wives devoted their lives to their homes and their children, but I didn't equate those things with love. I often heard women complaining about their husbands, and I sometimes heard husbands speak disparagingly of their wives. A few times I heard my friends' parents exchange hostile words, but when I reported those incidents to my mother, she told me she was sure they still loved each other. So really, what was love after all?

Sunday School lessons about loving my own family weren't easy to reconcile with my personal experience either. The stability of my parents' relationship grounded my life, and most of the time, I wanted to please them, but did that mean I *loved* them? My feelings toward my dad were warm and tender, but my feelings toward my mother were definitely mixed. She was often fun to be around, but she believed in firm discipline. Whenever she spanked me I was pretty sure I *hated* her.

My feelings toward my siblings were similarly ambivalent. Being constantly together for work, play, and general family life created a tight bond between us, but we certainly had our share of conflicts. My older sister was bossy, my younger sisters were annoying, and sometimes my brother was just plain mean. Whenever my brother made me really mad, I told him I wished he were dead, but those angry words always hung heavy in my heart. What if God actually granted my wish? As soon as I began to imagine life without my brother, I would start to cry. The underlying assurance that we all belonged to each other was deeply comforting, though I still didn't perceive those feelings as love.

The idea of loving my extended family was even more puzzling. Most of my relatives lived far away, so I barely knew them. I enjoyed spending time with a few cousins during our annual family reunions, but that didn't seem like love. My dad's mother was gentle and soft spoken, but she was really old, and I didn't know her well enough to think that I loved her. My mother's dad lived with us for most of my growing-up years, and I was sure I didn't love him. He was way too grouchy. And when he got into arguments with my mother, he frightened me.

Because I grew up in a secluded farming community, I knew few people from other towns, let alone other countries or cultures. Though my mother was from Australia, we didn't maintain much contact with relatives there after her father and brother came to live with us. As I mentioned in the fasting chapter, I actually did know something about children in China, because every time I didn't want to eat the food she put on my plate, Mother reminded me that they were starving. Unfortunately, her guilt tripping didn't engender love toward the suffering Chinese any more than it made me want to eat spinach or Swiss chard for dinner.

Also, growing up during the Cold War meant that I often heard conversations about how the Russians wanted to take over America. When airplanes flew overhead, I wondered if the Russians were coming to bomb us. Sometimes when I went to bed at night, I worried that they might be outside in the dark, waiting to take us prisoners. That certainly didn't engender good feelings toward foreign neighbors.

When I was seven or eight, an African-American family moved into a home on the far side of town. They had several children, but none of them were in my school class, so I had no close contact with them. I'd never seen a black person before, and whenever I saw someone from their family, all I could do was stare. They seemed so different. I remember being with my dad once when he engaged the parents in conversation, but I don't remember saying so much as a word to them. I can only guess how they must have felt, living in our remote, all-white, mostly Mormon community. They moved away in less than a year.

From the teachings I heard during my childhood, I gathered that loving others meant being *nice* to them. That usually meant making sacrifices I didn't want to make. It meant letting my little sister play with my special doll even if I didn't want her to. It meant letting someone else have the first turn on the swing every time. It meant giving part of my coveted treat to anyone who asked for it. It meant stopping what I was doing to fulfill someone else's wishes. It meant apologizing when I didn't really mean it. It meant doing whatever others wanted me to do so they didn't get upset. Loving others always seemed to give me the short end of the stick!

In spite of all the instruction I received about the importance of loving, I can remember being deliberately unkind, particularly to one of my little sisters and to a couple of my peers. It would seem logical that a child who felt as insecure and lacking as I did would reach out to those who had similar struggles, but for some reason, I was inclined to join the tormentors instead of offering kindness.

Even before I started elementary school, my insatiable desire for praise was busy building barriers to love. As the years went by, a sense of endless competition tainted all of my relationships. I was constantly comparing myself to others, always hoping, always striving, to be better than anyone else so I could win the praise prize. My competitiveness robbed me of the ability to enjoy the talents and gifts of others, and it left me forever critical of *everyone*. Though I sometimes tried to act as if I were happy for my siblings or peers when *they* received praise, I always felt diminished by their successes.

When anyone close to my age drew pictures, or sang, or threw a softball better than I did, I felt acutely inadequate. If a girl played the piano better than I did or got more blue ribbons at the county fair, I berated myself. When anyone in my classes got higher test scores than I did, I felt like a failure. In fact, I was only satisfied when I got a hundred percent on tests or assignments and no one else did.

But even succeeding according to my own standard caused anxiety, because then I worried that I might not measure up to future expectations.

Through college, mission, and early marriage, the habit of comparing myself and judging others continued, perpetuating my insecurities and inviting me to view everyone as my enemy. Though I desperately wanted acceptance, there was little room in my heart to nurture lasting friendships. I was too busy being fearful and trying to wheedle compliments out of every situation so that I could feel better about myself.

One thing that almost always made me feel better was serving others. Service made me feel like I was at least trying to following God's commandments, and it gave my troubled heart a positive sense of purpose. Nevertheless, I still had much to learn about the commandment to love my neighbor, because I was not nearly as concerned with helping others feel secure and happy as I was with soothing my own fears and feelings of inadequacy.

Christ says we must lose our lives to find them. Well, I was busily losing my life in service all right, but in reality, I had already lost my way in a mist of darkness. I was trying to save myself, hoping my willing service would somehow cancel—or at least conceal—my shortcomings, and propel me forward in my quest to become the perfect Molly Mormon. What a blessed moment it was when my humbled heart finally learned that if I would look to God instead of the arm of flesh, He would lead me to the genuine peace and love my spirit yearned for.

Today I gratefully rejoice in the love that constantly pours into my life.

On the day that I experienced God's total love and acceptance of *me personally*—exactly as I was, with all my fears, judgments, compulsiveness, and selfish desires—I was given a beautiful new frame of reference for loving others. As I felt His unconditional love replace my pain, I instantly loved Him in return, and somehow in that moment, a measure of His ability to love was transmitted into my own heart.

Without any conscious effort on my part, I suddenly felt a flood of unrestrained tenderness and compassion flowing from me to my son. The feeling quickly expanded to include his friends, and then expanded again to include others I'd never met. In that one pivotal moment, God—the source of all real love—taught me more about loving my neighbor than I had learned from all of my years of Sunday School classes and religion courses. When I felt God's total love for me, and my overflowing love for Him, I miraculously felt a general feeling of love for *everyone.*

This change of heart clearly sprang from God's pure love. It took away my fears and insecurities, bringing to a sudden end the fierce battle that had raged in my heart for so long. The barriers came crashing down as I experienced the truth that *we don't have to embrace each other's beliefs or behaviors to embrace each other.* I no longer felt I had to carefully weigh everything out to determine who it was safe or wise for me to love. There were no judgments to make, no fears to pacify. There was only love.

Tenderly, and oh, so beautifully, God showed me that loving my neighbor is fundamental to the life of freedom and joy that He wants for each of His children. At last I understood that this commandment had nothing to do with trying to force an elusive emotion into a resistant heart. Loving my neighbor means receiving pure, divine love. That pure love, by its very nature, gives me a sincere desire for others to receive the same blessings, advantages, and opportunities that I desire for myself. That love doesn't originate with me; it flows from Christ through me. It is an unfettered attitude of peace and goodwill. Angels rejoiced over the effects of Christ's love in those very words when they announced His birth to the shepherds: "glory to God in the highest and on earth peace, good will toward men."[1]

After God taught me the truth about love, I would often pause in wonder at what I was feeling inside, and at the way His love influenced my thoughts and interactions with others. My soul felt like it was smiling all the time! From this new vantage point, I could easily see why the first great commandment is to love God. Receiving and returning His love opened the way for me to understand and follow the second great commandment, to love my neighbor. I began to experience, at least in part, why Christ said that in loving God and others, my joy would be full.

Love allows me to appreciate and rejoice in the successes and accomplishments of others instead of feeling jealous, competitive or somehow diminished. Love helps me remember that we are all fellow travelers on a journey that is often stressful and difficult.

Love frees me to assume that everyone is doing the best they can, even when that may not appear to be the case.

Because of my natural woman condition, little skirmishes still arise in my heart from time to time. When I feel my love faltering, I usually turn to God and say something like, "Okay, I know *You* love this person, but *I'm* not feeling much love for him right now. I really want to, but I'm really not. Would You please let me borrow from Your infinite supply of love to make up the difference?" His response is usually immediate. A feeling of good will flows to me, and my heart is softened. Clearly, God is eager to help me replace that spirit of contention and judgment with the spirit of love, peace, and compassion.

For many years, I didn't realize how important love is. I used to think that temple attendance was the key to returning to God's presence. Today I have come to understand that while temple covenants and ordinances may be essential, I cannot enter the presence of God unless I am filled with His pure love, having become one with Him in His love for all of His children.

Only a truly loving heart can abide His holiness. Temple recommend questions that ask about how we treat family members and our fellowmen are evidence that having a testimony, sustaining our leaders, and obeying the Word of Wisdom are not enough. Our lives must also bear the bounteous fruits of love.

Since those early movie days, I've learned that love isn't the all-about-me feeling I thought it was, although it is indeed an amazing, wonderful feeling. I've also come to understand that love is a verb—an act or attitude of true kindness. To that, I would add that love is a *choice, a decision*. It is a choice motivated by a desire to live in the freedom, peace, and joy that Christ offers His humble followers.

Choosing love is a decision I must make over and over and over again, every single day. Sometimes it's an easy, almost instinctive choice. However, sometimes I have to mentally stop myself in the middle of a situation and make a conscious decision to think and act lovingly. Such moments bring to mind the expression Alma used when he counseled his son Corianton to stand firm against temptation. Alma said, "Cross yourself in these things."[2]

The phrase "cross yourself" gives me a sense of suspending time so that I can *cross examine* my motives and impulses. It means I refrain from acting until I consider my options. Am I willing to do the work required to bring love to a challenging situation, or am I going to take the tempting, natural woman path of criticism and judgment? Crossing myself gives me a chance to consider the consequences of different thoughts and actions. It allows me to seek the strength and guidance of the Holy Ghost in making choices that will lead to peace and joy.

Of course, I'm aware that I haven't even begun to master the art of loving as Christ loves; I'm just an eager apprentice. But He has shown me the way, and He gently entreats me to follow. As I've humbly and prayerfully sought to do so, His grace has attended my efforts—even though sometimes they're rather feeble—bringing an abundance of peace and joy into my life.

The glorious gift of love that came as a result of my change of heart experience transformed my feelings about my son and gave me a beautiful new way to relate to him. Since that day, God's gift of love has left its mark on countless situations and circumstances that I've encountered. Though less dramatic than my original change of heart experience, they continually remind me that a life filled with love is a joyful life.

Some time ago our internet wasn't working. I called our provider, and a repairman arrived at my door. After some testing, he said that the problem was in the junction box in our neighbor's backyard. He left to make the repair but quickly returned, telling me that when he started to open the gate, he got a definite "do not enter" warning from a large, threatening dog. Our neighbors weren't home to take the dog inside, so he said I would need to arrange something with them before the internet problem could be resolved. For a moment I was tempted to let him know how frustrated I was at the prospect of being without e-mail for another day, but I quickly dismissed those thoughts and instead thanked him for his quick response.

That evening I called my neighbor and explained the situation. Her words were abrupt and decisive. She said she and her husband were both working every day for the next several weeks, and that the dog would tear up the house if she left him inside, so, sorry, she couldn't help me.

Oh, baby, did my natural woman ever kick in!

She obviously doesn't care if I ever have internet or e-mail again! If the shoe were on the other foot, I'd surely figure out some way to help her. How can she be so ...

Just as I was about to continue my mental tirade, the Spirit invited me to "cross myself." In that moment I suddenly remembered how much I admire this woman, how dedicated she has been to her work with special-needs children, how many troubled family members she has anchored and influenced for good, and how her words often sound much tougher than she really is. As my agitated heart softened, I was immediately filled with love, respect, and compassion.

"Gosh," I said to her. "I'm sorry things are so stressful for you right now. I didn't realize your husband is still working. I thought he retired last fall."

The tone of our call completely changed. She told me her husband had gone back to work and that he had been having some health challenges. She also shared some of the challenges she faced in managing the care of her father who had moved in with her ten years earlier at about the same time my mother had moved in with us. After discussing some of the challenges of meeting aging parents' needs, our conversation began to wind down. Before we hung up she offered to take the dog to her son's house the next day so our internet could be repaired. Even though doing so would require extra effort and inconvenience on her part, she assured me that she was happy to do it.

After saying goodbye to her, I looked heavenward, raised my arms in praise to God, and thanked Him aloud for yet another love miracle.

My internet was working before ten o'clock the next morning, but far more importantly, my relationship with my neighbor remained warm and supportive. Indeed, my love and appreciation for her actually increased as a result of this experience.

As is undoubtedly the case for most people, volumes could be written about situations that have arisen in my home requiring me to choose between love and frustration. When I pause to consider what is happening below the surface of each conflict, it always seems to boil down to one question: Will I respond with a heart at peace, or will I respond with a heart at war?[3]

I have to make this choice each time I reach for a utensil from a kitchen cabinet and find that it was put away without being properly cleaned. At that point, I can choose to be irritated that my mother has "done it again," or I can tenderly consider how much she wants to serve our family even though her eyes are growing dim, and she can't always tell whether a spoon, or a bowl, or a pan has been thoroughly cleaned. When I notice muddy footprints tracked through the house, I have a similar choice to make. Even if I don't say anything, my choice to embrace love rather than war has a profound influence on how I feel.

When I open the fridge and something crashes to the floor and makes a sticky mess, love choices again present themselves. Do I look for someone to blame—surely *I* didn't leave that bottle of syrup so precariously perched—or do I reach for the cleaning supplies as I thank God for the people I'm privileged to share my home with? (Actually, I've done both on different occasions and there's no question which choice I prefer living with when all is said and done.)

One sweet result of choosing love toward others is that I find myself being patient with my own mistakes—often even laughing at them—instead of feeling irritated, distressed, condemning, or otherwise critical of myself. It's a fun way to live. I've paused to thank God for this joyful blessing many, many times. It is such a lovely change from how I used to live.

Opportunities to choose a loving path are everywhere. Recently as I was preparing dinner for guests who were about to arrive, I found that I needed to make a quick dash to the grocery store. As I drove into the parking lot, I had to wait for no fewer than seven people to cross in front of me. Three of them dawdled shamelessly, backtracking more than once to taunt and tease each other. It would have been the perfect time to stew over how inconsiderate they were, but instead, a spirit of love invited me to cross myself, enjoy their camaraderie, and imagine how much fun it would be to get to know the bearded guy in the black-and-white floral pants. After all, I was wearing my tan, red, and black pants that hint of African folk art. We might really hit it off!

Crossing myself and choosing love has also been a blessing in my church callings, whether dealing with an irate parent over a girls' camp policy, a frustrated sister over a bishop's storehouse regulation, an upset scout leader who felt I should have handled something differently, or a number of other sticky situations. In the presence of love, intense feelings have given way to understanding and forgiveness, restoring feelings of cooperation, support and good will.

Even when things don't come to a perfect resolution, I'm better able to come to a place of peace when I've sought the Spirit and done what I could to bring love to the situation. Whenever I've chosen something other than love, I've found myself left with regret and the prompting that I need to apologize for my actions.

My need to make love choices will last as long as life itself. I'm so glad I've learned that making the choice to be loving opens the doorway of my heart to the feelings I most desire. Admittedly, situations do occasionally arise which cannot be lightly dismissed, but ultimately, I believe that a loving heart will always be my best asset. Dwelling on frustration never solves the problem, and it robs me of the delicious fruits of love.

Before developing my new understanding, I thought yielding to love meant yielding to the wishes of others—that if I were to be truly loving, I would never be able to have or do what *I* wanted. Now I understand that while good relationships usually do require an element of compromise, maintaining a feeling of peace and goodwill doesn't require sacrificing good judgment or my preferences. In fact, I've learned it can often be quite the opposite.

Sometimes establishing specific boundaries has been my only hope for bringing love to a troubled relationship. When I start to feel resentful or otherwise unloving, I often notice a boundary problem that needs to be dealt with. Receiving the Spirit's guidance during this process is essential. Appropriate boundaries can be challenging to establish, but my prayerful efforts have been greatly rewarded. Such has been the case with employees who have repeatedly asked for money in advance, with children who want inappropriate privileges, with friends and extended family members who expect unreasonable favors.

Sometimes the most loving thing I can do is to clear my heart of judgment and fear, and simply say, "No," or perhaps a softened, "I'm sorry. That doesn't work for me." I've been blessed to watch appropriate boundary setting salvage rocky marriage relationships and fill them with renewed love and respect. This is a topic I'm passionate about for many reasons, but I won't belabor it here. If you are interested, you can find more on boundaries in the appendix.

Realizing that God focuses on the present has relieved much of the stress I used to feel about the commandment to love everyone. He provides the guidance that is needed in the moment—not what I may need in a hypothetical situation tomorrow, next week, or ten years from now. I don't have to worry about whether I can love everyone all the time. I just need to allow him to show me the loving thing I need to think or do *right now*.

When I walk in the light of His love, He fills my heart with love, and He guides me in handling each situation as it arises. To His disciples Christ said, "Take no thought how or what ye shall speak,"[4] promising that the Spirit would give them the appropriate words as they needed them. I've noticed that the more I relax and trust Him to fill my heart and words with His love, the more He fulfills that promise.

As I continue to ponder the profound impact love has had on my life, love seems to be not just *one* of the virtues, but rather the wellspring of *all* virtues. Perhaps that explains why Christ identified love for God and love for our neighbor as the two laws on which all other laws hang. I believe that if we could see things as they really are, we would discover that love holds the solution to all of the troubles of the world.

I'm a patriotic American who cherishes the freedoms our flag represents, but my primary allegiance is to God, not to my country, or even to my religion—though I feel deeply loyal to both. Above all other distinctions, I'm first and foremost a member of God's great family, sustained by His infinite love. Regardless of national origins or religious beliefs, we're all in this life together. God has given each of us different gifts. He intends for us to enjoy one another's gifts and bless one another's lives with them. The natural man entices us to create divisions, but God repeatedly entreats us to become one, not only with Him, but with one another.

Today my life is enriched beyond measure by awesome friends who hail from many lands scattered across the globe: Central and South America, Finland, Austria, Australia, Germany, Puerto Rico, Haiti, Africa, Canada, Denmark, Ireland, Japan, and who-knows-where-all else! I rejoice in the universality of our divine heritage and in our common desires for peace and happiness. As I've learned to approach our differences with an open heart, God has helped me create beautiful bonds of love, appreciation, and delight with countless friends.

When Nephi was being tutored by an angel, he was asked if he knew the meaning of the tree that his father, Lehi, had been shown. Nephi responded, "Yea, it is the love of God, which sheddeth itself abroad in the hearts of the children of men; wherefore, it is the most desirable above all things." The angel confirmed that Nephi's answer was correct, but then went on to add another glorious truth. "Yea, and the most *joyous* to the soul."[5]

Apparently the angel wanted Nephi to expand his understanding to include the *joy* love brings to the soul. That is also my witness. Over and over I have been blessed to feel the incredible joy of God's love deep within my soul.

You may not be surprised to know that from time to time, I've been accused of being an incorrigible Pollyanna. But really, is it any wonder that I'm so in love with love? It lifted the dark clouds that engulfed my soul, opened my heart, and gave me a new life! With that new life came a deep desire to enjoy the constant companionship of the Spirit of God. That blessing can only be attained by loving God *and* loving my neighbor. Regardless of what I have to do, love must be at the foundation. It must be in and through all that I do, guiding me in what I do, and how I do it.

Loving my neighbor is really "where the rubber meets the road." It's what all of my scripture study, prayer, fasting, temple attendance, and churchgoing is about—to learn to love as Christ loves, first the Father and then His children. Some of Mormon's final and most powerful words say, "If ye have not charity, ye are nothing." Then he counsels Christ's followers to "Pray unto the Father with all the energy of heart that ye may be filled with this love … that when he shall appear we shall be like him."[6] My hope is to be like Him.

I've been given a unique set of circumstances that provide me with endless opportunities to develop a loving nature. If I don't diligently seek to increase my ability to love my neighbor, nothing else I do is ultimately going to matter.

I'll never be able to adequately express my gratitude to God for His gift of love, which lifted me from the rut of perfectionism, fear, and judging, and gently placed me in the groove of peace, faith, and joy.

It's a glorious place to live!

CONCLUSION

I GLORY IN MY JESUS!

From Wretched to Rejoicing

My final confession ... I confess that "I glory in my Jesus"

The phrase "walking in darkness at noon-day"[1] is a perfect description of the way I lived my life for far too many years. Truth was all around me, and yet I was so encumbered with my Molly Mormon fears and perfectionism that I wasn't able to embrace it. Although I experienced many happy times with my family during childhood, and later with my husband and children, my deep-seated, false beliefs always drew me back to a place of fear and judgment.

The seven confessions I've made here are by no means all that I could admit to. I could write other chapters about my feelings of shame for being afraid to share the gospel, my feelings of guilt and despair regarding family home evening, my feelings of dishonesty over testimony bearing, my feelings of inadequacy in my callings, my feelings of disappointment that paying my tithing never brought me unexpected money like it did for others, and so on.

My mistaken perceptions about the nature of God, along with my drive to perfect myself, blinded me to many truths, and also to the endless stream of divine love which God intended for me to depend on through the challenges I faced. Consequently, my reality was framed against a constricting backdrop of fear and judgment instead of an expanding backdrop of hope and love.

With my change of heart, Christ gave me beauty for ashes, just as He promised He would.[2] Is it any wonder I so passionately adore Him today? He freed me from my frenzied mindset—my fear-based determination to perfect myself—and He continues to free me from my fears today. With Nephi I gratefully proclaim, "*I glory in my Jesus, for he hath redeemed my soul from hell.*"[3]

Often I shake my head in wonder at the beliefs that once created such havoc in my life. Why did I allow them to invade my thinking and crowd out the peace and hope Christ held out to me? Why wasn't I more receptive to the Spirit? It's very tempting to look back and wonder how different my life might have been if only I had understood the truth of God's love from the beginning. Would I have been a more obedient daughter? A more loving wife? A more patient mother? Would my children have had fewer problems to deal with? Would I have been a better influence for good in the Church and in my community all these years?

Unlike George Bailey in *It's a Wonderful Life*, no one can really know the answers to hypothetical questions about the past. But the truth is, no one *needs* to know. Life is about moving forward, or, to again borrow from Nephi's words, it is about "press[ing] forward with a steadfastness in Christ, having a perfect brightness of hope, and a love of God and of all men."[4] Life is about today. It's being created in this very moment. This day is not for regretting; it's for loving, learning, and rejoicing. If I'm always looking back at yesterday, I miss the joy God offers me *today*.

Besides, I don't have to worry. Christ has everything covered. That is what His Atonement is all about. Didn't He give the worker who started in the field in the eleventh hour the same reward as the worker who started in the first hour?[5] He heals broken hearts *whenever* they are placed on His altar.

He says, "Search diligently, pray always, and be believing, and all things shall work together for your good."[6] When He says "all things," I believe He means *all* things. That includes my years of bulimia, my depression, my compulsiveness, my judging, my suffering over my beloved son, my perfectionism—all of it!

It includes my character flaws that can still send me momentarily chasing after Molly Mormon illusions. This is Christ's miracle: He makes me enough when I give Him my heart. His mission is to do for those who love Him what we cannot do for ourselves. He loves us more than He loved His own life, more than all the glory the world could ever offer. Now *that's* true love!

When my heart is filled with love, I can easily find reasons to rejoice even though I'm not particularly pleased with how things are going at the moment. That doesn't mean I speak lightly or flippantly about rejoicing when I'm in pain, or when someone else is struggling, but it does mean I can live my life from day to day in the light of hope.

I often remind myself that I'm engaged in a mortal, natural-woman experience, with all the human weakness intrinsic to this earthly existence. Though I certainly don't understand all things, this much I do know: God loves all of His children with a perfect love. He can and will make all things work together for my good as I turn to Him.

If I notice that I'm falling short of the love and the loveliness I desire, I now know there is no reason to despair. My beloved

Savior understands. By turning to Him in faith and inviting my natural woman to yield to the enticings of His Spirit, I can receive the courage to let go of my fears and reject the enticings of this mortal world. My heart is then open to accept His redeeming grace—His amazing power to make me whole—instead of being torn and fragmented by worldly cares.

When distress and frustration do sneak up on me, a passage from Nephi often helps me regain my perspective and my sense of humor. I call it "my wretched woman scripture." Nephi says he "delights in the things of the Lord," but when he ponders on his weakness he cries out, "Oh wretched man that I am."[7]

Like Nephi, my soul delights in the things of the Lord, yet moments arise when I feel anything but delighted, oh wretched woman that I am! My head still knows that all things will work together for my good, but my heart isn't feeling it right then.

During such a time, if my husband happens to call from work and ask how my day is going I'll most likely respond, "It's a wretched woman day!" And then we both laugh. From that one little statement he knows that I'm grappling with some unnamed challenge, but he also knows I'm tenaciously clinging to Nephi's words that follow: "*Nevertheless*, I *know* in whom I have trusted. My *God* hath been my support."[8]

Whether or not I offer more details about the situation, my husband understands that I'm looking to Christ as my Rock and my Rescuer.

The story of my transformation from a fearful Molly Mormon to a joyful Molly Mortal is largely encompassed in a concept that I heard taught by Chauncey Riddle, a former BYU professor.[9] He identified the "outer gospel" as the physical, visible, measurable things we do as we practice our religion.

These actions can be "seen of men." Things like reading the scriptures, praying (particularly in public), going to church, paying tithing, and even taking the sacrament fit into this category. They readily lend themselves to lists, but they don't have the power in and of themselves to bring me to Christ.

The things of the "inner gospel" are the workings of the heart, and they're visible only to God. They must be added to my outer gospel practices to bring me to Christ. Things like pondering the emblems of the sacrament, confessing my weakness to God, and committing to be more Christlike are part of the inner gospel. Earnestly seeking the Spirit to increase my understanding of a scripture passage, turning to Christ with a sincere desire to trust Him when I'm troubled, humbly praying for strength and guidance in the face of adversity, following daily promptings, rejoicing in His amazing love—all of these and so much more belong to the inner gospel. Other people can't discern whether I'm living the inner gospel—that's between God and me—but as I do my best to live the inner gospel, my heart remains soft and open to God.

In a recent regional conference, one of the speakers made a statement that instantly caught my attention. He said, "Some people believe there is too much busyness going on in the Church. It *is possible* to go to church year after year and never find the gospel." That was exactly the tragedy of my life. I was busily—frantically—*doing* my religion, diligently trying to live the outer gospel. But I found no lasting peace, no joy, no happiness in the "good news" of the gospel of Jesus Christ *until I started internalizing its glorious truths by living the inner gospel.* When I relinquished my Molly Mormon fears, I was suddenly more available to receive the promptings of the Spirit. With His help, my practice of the inner gospel *and* the outer gospel shifted into harmony with each other. Both are essential to bring the kingdom of heaven to earth.

In my early years, the commandment to "be ye therefore perfect"[10] was a huge stumbling block for me. In my mind, "perfect" meant "flawless." The commandment stood in complete opposition to the obvious, since no mortal is flawless. Over and over I heard people say, "Nobody's perfect. There was only one perfect person, and that was Christ."

Being perfect was clearly an absolutely unattainable goal—I was a hundred percent assured of failure—and yet I thought I was supposed to work my tail off trying to reach it. To console those of us who found that frustrating, teachers would sometimes say, "You can't be perfect in *everything*, but you can be perfect in one or two small things. Strive to become perfect in just one small way." Was that really supposed to make my massive failure feel somehow less painful?

There was much joy and rejoicing in my heart when I used LDS view and found alternate translations of the Greek word for "perfect." It means complete, finished, or fully developed.[11] Those words don't make me feel like I have to frantically strive to reach an impossible goal. They seem to invite me to expand my possibilities and become more than I already am, without implying that I'm somehow not good enough for God (and probably never will be).

Alternate translations of one of the Hebrew words for *perfect* are complete, whole, having integrity.[12] The concept of wholeness feels even more joyful to me. Wholeness was what I felt that day when God immersed me in His love. There was no illusion of flawlessness, but I still sensed that every part of me was acceptable to Him, that I was beautifully whole in my present state. No part of me was fragmented or rejected in any way.

Wholeness is what I feel when I capture a scripture and a feeling of peace and love floods over me. It's what I feel when a prayer of gratitude swells in my heart and expands throughout my being until it presses tears from my eyes.

To some, these alternate translations may seem like splitting hairs, but to me, they are another manifestation of God's love and compassion. They witness that my battle with perfectionism belongs in Christ's hands rather than in my heart. He alone can make me feel complete and whole. When I give Him my heart, His mercy covers my inadequacy.

Though I don't feel "whole" all the time, when I do feel fragmented, adrift on the turbulent sea of life, I know what to do; I know where to go. There is a safe harbor. Returning to Christ each day anchors my life with hope and joy.

After Jesus performed the miracle of feeding the five thousand, people came to Him hoping He'd give them more bread. Instead of feeding them again, He told them that *He* was the bread of life and that they needed to eat His flesh and drink His blood if they truly wanted to be filled. That wasn't at all what they wanted to hear, and the scriptures say that "from that time many of his disciples went back, and walked no more with him." At that point Jesus turned to the apostles and asked, "Will ye also go away?"[13]

I absolutely love Peter's humble response. It begins with a question we've probably all asked ourselves, and ends with his testimony born of experience and faith. "*Lord, to whom shall we go? thou hast the words of eternal life.* And we believe and are sure that thou art that Christ, the Son of the living God."[14]

Like Peter, my experience has taught me that there truly is no one better to turn to. There is absolutely no Rock like the Savior.

Through His love, my fearful, perfectionistic heart continues to be changed to a believing heart.

I believe Him when He says, "it is not requisite that a [woman] should run faster than [she] has strength."[15] In other words, I don't have to do every good thing that pops into my head. I don't have to make endless lists so I don't forget anything. It's not my job to perfect myself through my works. Perfection is beyond my own strength. It is Christ's wondrous atoning grace that makes it possible for me to rejoice in God's presence rather than shrink from it.

The impossible has been replaced with the doable! I no longer doubt that I will one day enjoy celestial glory, not because I am so good, but because Christ is so GOOD. He is so merciful. I love Him with all my heart—or at least as the sacrament prayer says, I am *willing* to.

I know I can trust His words when He says, "Eye hath not seen, nor ear heard, neither have entered into the heart of man, the things which God hath prepared for them that love him."[16] Interestingly, though, the thought of some far future reward is no longer my focal point. My aim is to fill my life with His love in each moment so I can live in His joy—in His presence—as much as possible *today*. I'm completely confident the rest will follow.

My journey has taught me that there is simply no substitute for the nurturing power of God's love. Just as I must eat frequently to sustain the strength of my physical body, I must receive God's love frequently, preferably always, for my spirit to remain strong.

My journey has also taught me that the Lord offers many avenues—many commandments—for me to be nourished by His love. For years I mistook them for measuring sticks that would be used during a severe final judgment. Now I know they are actually a treasured set of keys God wants me to use to unlock the sweetness of His presence in my life today.

That Molly Mormon urge to rush around, trying to do more than is humanly possible to qualify for the celestial kingdom, no longer haunts my life. Christ has redeemed my soul from the hell I lived in when fear controlled my life. It has been replaced with a glorious sense of peace and joy.

That doesn't mean I never rush around trying to fit more into a day than is reasonable. I'm still a "doer." I love serving others, I love to talk to people, I love to plan and prepare, and I love to do things on the spur of the moment.

However, during quiet moments of reflection and meditation, which I also love, I'm reminded that my doing isn't what makes me "good enough" to live in God's presence. My actions have never been enough, and they never could be enough. It's my loyal, ever-present love for God, for His children, and for the Savior, coupled with His mercy and His perfect love that becomes enough.

When Christ says, "Come unto me," I *want* to come. When He says, "Learn of me, and listen to my words; walk in the meekness of my Spirit," I want to do those things with all my heart. When He says, "You shall have peace in me," I believe Him. I know He will show me how to live in the light of His love if I come to Him. He is full of mercy, but I must offer Him my heart. Otherwise, He cannot make me whole.[17]

I'm grateful I can turn to God and expect to feel His companionship and guidance. Sometimes waiting on the Lord *is* necessary, but I'm amazed at how many answers and tender mercies come quickly when I watch for them and keep myself open to receive His subtle surprises.

My gospel maxim used to be, "Life is a test," suggesting that life was *supposed* to be hard and that by enduring years of difficulty, I would eventually prove myself worthy to live with Him. Now that I have a better understanding of Christ and His devotion to each of the Father's children, my new gospel maxim has become, "The password is joy!"

Life is meant to be joyful.

I don't deny that there must be pain and sorrow along life's path. Sometimes it is overwhelming. As followers of Christ that is to be expected. But I truly believe "men are, that they might have joy."[18] Joy comes through Christ's love, and He is eager to help me fill my life with His love this very day, this very moment. His merciful, amazing love is the power that continually enables me to trade my perfectionism for peace, my fear for faith, and my judging for joy.

APPENDIX

In this appendix I have included additional material relating to each of my seven confessions. Some of these entries are referred to in the main text of this book. Others are here because they were cut from the main text for one reason or another, but I still wanted to make them available to the reader. Some of the journal entries have been edited for clarity.

1. God and His Tattletale Angels

A more detailed description of my transforming encounter with God's love—my change of heart experience—can be found in my article titled *You Just Have to Love*, which is available on my website at www.ElonaShelley.com.

I'm currently working on another book that offers more details of my journey from childhood innocence to later despair and finally to joy. I hope to have it ready for publication in 2014. Its availability will be noted on the above website.

My friend's change of heart experience

A dear friend of mine experienced a sudden change of heart during a very difficult time in her life. When she was informed that her husband had a terminal brain tumor, she was overwhelmed with anxiety and fear. For several days she mentally reviewed all the problems his death would create for her and their children. The prospects felt like more than she could bear. After a while she noticed that the words, "Trust in the Lord with all thy heart," frequently interrupted her endless stream of fearful thoughts. Finally she paused to wonder if the Lord might be trying to tell her something.

She got her scriptures and located those words in Proverbs. "Trust in the LORD with all thine heart; and lean not unto thine own understanding. In all thy ways acknowledge him, and he shall direct thy paths."[1] As she reflected on the message of those two short verses, her fears were replaced with a sweet sense of peace. She felt a profound, comforting assurance that God loved her, and that he also loved her husband and children. Suddenly she knew beyond any doubt that whatever happened—regardless of how hard it might be to endure—it would truly be the very best thing for their family.

This experience with God's love strengthened her throughout the surgeries and treatments her husband received during the remaining two years of his life. Whenever bad news came following periods of improvement, she would catch herself being tempted to slip back into despair. However, by remembering this experience, she was able to return to a place of peace. She said she sometimes felt guilty when people asked her how she was doing, because she often felt joy rather than sadness. She attributes her continued peace to the change of heart she received from the Lord that day.

Occasionally my friend and I have discussed what it was that made the difference for each of us. We both recognize that the change in our hearts happened the moment we felt the absolute reality of God's unfailing love. It was not enough to know *about*

God's love. We had to *feel* it to experience that change. Perhaps that explains why Sister Parkins, the former General Relief Society President, said, "If I could have one thing happen for every woman in this Church, it would be that they would feel the love of the Lord in their lives daily."[2] I wonder if *feeling* God's love was also at the foundation of the mighty change that Alma, Paul, Enos, Nephi and others experienced.

2. Using the Iron Rod as a Weapon of Self-Destruction

Understanding more about repentance

Repentance is an amazing gospel principle that is often misunderstood. Because I have come to see this gift as a priceless treasure, I have chosen to include a few entries about it here.

My early feelings about repentance

When I was young, the word "repent" had a very negative connotation to me. I thought it meant you had to feel guilty for the bad things you'd done, and then figure out how to get God to forgive you by praying and suffering. I had the idea that the amount of guilt and suffering had to match the seriousness of the sin, and that after you'd suffered *enough*, God would finally forgive you. One of my big problems with repentance was that I didn't know how to determine when I had suffered enough to be forgiven!

I knew if you did something *really* bad, you had to make an appointment to talk to the bishop so he knew about it too. That seemed like it would be terribly embarrassing, but at least he might be able to help you know when you had suffered enough for God to forgive you.

Repentance wasn't something I wanted to do, but I knew it was something I needed to do. In fact, I did so many bad things that I wasn't ever sure which sin was the most important one to be working on. I was good at feeling guilty for being bad, but even when I prayed about being sorry for a certain sin, I didn't know if God really forgave me. I wondered if my attempts to repent got anything erased or if those angels were just chalking up more and more bad stuff on my heavenly slate. I was afraid I would never remember everything I was supposed to repent of.

I was also taught that if you repented of something but then you did the same thing again, all the bad stuff God had wiped off your slate earlier automatically jumped back onto it.

Shades of these concepts (usually in more mature terminology) came with me into adulthood. In my mind, repentance was pretty much a necessary evil.

As with so many other things, my change of heart experience opened the way for me to understand beautiful new truths about repentance. Now I understand what people were talking about years ago when I heard them say they repented every day. Like them, I find great joy in repenting by returning my focus to Christ every day.

And I no longer believe what I was taught about all my sins returning if I mess up in the same way again. I believe *Christ* when He says, "As often as *my people* repent will I forgive them their trespasses against me."[3] I've felt that forgiveness, along with His desire for me to continue repenting and finding joy in becoming more like Him.

However, I believe it is important to note what Christ also says in the very next verse: "And ye shall also forgive one another your trespasses." In the Sermon on the Mount, He explains that we can't expect the Father to forgive us if we don't forgive one another.[4]

So now I've come full circle. God is eager to forgive me as I repent, but I must forgive others if I am to be forgiven. I need to focus on keeping my covenants with God so that He can claim me as one of "His people" who are forgiven as often as they repent.

I seek His help in forgiving others so that He will forgive me. I also seek to learn from my experiences. Like a baby learning to walk, I get up and try again, knowing that I will again fall, but also knowing that a loving Father is there to support me in the learning process.

When I view "sin" as anything that takes me away from Christ, and repentance as the process of returning to Christ, I can experience the challenges of life without a mountain of unnecessary guilt and shame weighing me down. Though the Lord uses guilt and shame to help us stay on track, He doesn't expect us to carry it around endlessly. He is eager to take them from us as we are willing to turn and give them to Him.

Thoughts on Repentance

Journal entry January 2008: I have always loved the song, "Oh, That I Were an Angel,"[5] but before my change of heart, the message of this song and the scripture it is based on[6] made me feel despairingly guilty. I didn't have any desire to cry repentance to *anyone*, much less "every people." Each time I heard that the mission of the church was to call the world to repentance, I cringed. Telling people, whether friends or strangers, that they were sinners and that they needed to repent seemed like a very intimidating duty—as if I didn't have any sins I needed to repent of myself!

Today it hit me that since my new understanding of repentance is "turning to Christ," calling someone to repentance could actually mean *inviting them* to turn to Christ. *Crying* repentance seems like it would mean testifying with all the energy of my heart. Fulfilling my responsibility to cry repentance, then, could include gladly bearing witness of the joy I have found in following Christ's teachings. Today it's easy for me to bear that witness.

LDS View: A great help for studying gospel principles like repentance.

(For a free copy of LDS View see note 5 of chapter 1. To learn how to use LDS View, go to the "Getting Started Tutorial" on the Help menu.)

I love having LDS View available when I'm studying the scriptures. Although I prefer to read and study the scriptures in printed form, sometimes I need to look something up in LDS View. Then I end up on my computer for the rest of my study time, pondering and searching as thoughts and questions come to my mind.

Since the principle of repentance is so dear to my heart, I decided I would study that topic using LDS View and share my experience, detail by detail. At the end of my study time, my capturing seemed to naturally turn into a written prayer. If you remember, Colleen Harrison said that often happens.

Okay, so I begin by entering the word *repent* into the search box. I find that it occurs 46 times in the Old Testament, 66 in the New Testament, 362 in the Book of Mormon, 129 in the

Doctrine and Covenants, and 25 in the Pearl of Great Price. (Each occurrence of the word is highlighted in a box containing a few lines before and a few lines after the word.)

I scroll though the references in the Old Testament, and notice that the word *repent* is often used to mean that a person or God is basically changing his mind about something. A few verses have the more traditional connotation of someone coming back to God after straying, but most of the verses seem to have a less spiritual meaning. When I click on the New Testament, I scroll through the verses and find the more traditional connotation of *forsaking sin and coming back to Christ.*

I've already studied this words numerous times. More than once I've used the Hebrew and Greek dictionaries of the LDS View Resource Edition to look for other translations of the words which have been most commonly translated as *repent* or *repentance.* The Hebrew words usually mean *being sorry or having pity.* But when I clicked on Ezekiel 14:6 I find that the Hebrew word for repent in that verse means *to turn back.* In this case, the scripture in English says, "Thus sayeth the Lord God; Repent, and turn yourselves from your idols." That's the definition that has spoken to my heart in recent years: basically, turn away from the world and turn back to Christ.

In the dictionary box is also a long list of all the ways this word was translated in the King James Version of the Bible. None of them catch my eye. I often find a note at the bottom that gives more information and clarification about the word, but there isn't one in this case.

After a little more scanning of the Old Testament, I decide to go to the New Testament. Here I repeatedly find translations from the Greek that mean to *think differently* or *reconsider.* The note at the bottom says this Greek word denotes a 'change of heart or mind', i.e. 'a conversion.' That doesn't have the heavy negative connotation I knew in my childhood. Where did that come from anyway? Did teachers think we would behave better if we were afraid to sin because repentance was so formidable?

Another definition I commonly find is *compunction* (for guilt, including *reformation*); by implication *reversal* (of [another's] decision). Hmmm! I wonder if "the reversal of another's decision" could mean the reversal of God's decision to exclude us from his presence. (Actually I think it's the law of justice that excludes us, because God has to honor that law unless we repent so Christ can pay the price of justice, that is, redeem us.) That's a cool thought. Repentance is the gospel principle which allows the atonement to purify our hearts so we can enter God's presence.

Monte recently told me that he sometimes finds cool insights in the English Guide to the Scriptures, which is only available in electronic versions. I go back to the first page, select the study helps, type in *repent* and find the following explanation.

> **Repent, Repentance.** A change of mind and heart that brings a fresh attitude toward God, oneself, and life in general. Repentance implies that a person turns away from evil and turns his heart and will to God, submitting to God's commandments and desires and forsaking sin. True repentance comes from a love for God and a sincere desire to obey his commandments. All accountable persons have sinned and must repent in order to progress toward salvation. Only through the atonement of Jesus Christ can our repentance become effective and accepted by God.

That's sound awesome! I especially like the part that says, "True repentance comes from a love for God and a sincere desire to obey his commandments." I wonder if it says the same thing in the Bible Dictionary, so I look up the entry for repent. I find it doesn't use the same wording. As I look through it, I realize that the two entries contain approximately the same information, but the Guide to the Scriptures speaks more to my heart. The Bible Dictionary sounds more factual and academic to me.

Oh, and I notice that the Guide to the Scriptures says repentance is "a change of mind *and heart* that brings a fresh *attitude* toward God." The Bible Dictionary doesn't mention *heart,* and it uses the word *view* rather than *attitude.*

I can tell there's a lot to ponder in those two entries. I'd like to capture each of them sometime, but for now I just copy and paste them into a new document for later consideration.

Right now I want to look at the New Testament occurrences of repentance. Going back to the search results, I see the first entry is Matthew 3:1–3. "In those days came John the Baptist, preaching in the wilderness of Judæa, And saying, *Repent ye: for the kingdom of heaven is at hand."*

I scroll past the next two occurrences of *repentance* which are words of John the Baptist and stop on Matthew 4:17 where John's exact words are spoken by Jesus. It says, "Jesus began to preach, and to say, *Repent: for the kingdom of heaven is at hand."* I expand the window so I can see what the earlier verses are about and see that these words come immediately after Matthew's account of Jesus fasting forty days and then prevailing over Satan's temptations.

I scroll through a few other occurrences until I come to Mark 1:5 and notice that in this account, Christ says, "*The time is fulfilled, and the kingdom of God is at hand: repent ye, and believe the gospel."*

I decide to check the other gospels to see if I can find a similar quote. In Luke, the first two occurrences are again about John the Baptist. I scroll through the twelve other occurrences of *repent* in Luke, expanding them here and there to see what Christ is talking about each time. (I'm surprised to note that there are no occurrences in the gospel of John.)

When I expand Luke 17:3, verses 3 and 4 catch my attention. "Take heed to yourselves: If thy brother trespass against thee, rebuke him; and if he repent, forgive him. And if he trespass against thee seven times in a day, and seven times in a day turn again to thee, saying, I repent; thou shalt forgive him."

Hey, that first part sounds like it could be used in the appendix material for chapter 7 that I was working on earlier today! It's about setting boundaries and it says that when something bothers you, you are responsible to communicate your expectations and feelings instead of blaming others for your unhappiness. The *Boundaries* book even uses the example of *trespassing* on someone else's property.

Now, thinking about the word r*ebuke,* it seems pretty aggressive. In my mind, rebuking someone would be more likely to perpetuate a problem than to resolve it. I wonder if there's an alternate translation for rebuke that makes more sense.

To answer that question I venture into the more intimidating Resource Edition of LDS View. There I find that the word translated *rebuke* means *censure* or *admonish.* So Christ expects me to censure or admonish someone if they offend me? (Wait, does transgress mean *offend?* Let me check that in the Greek Dictionary real quick.)

Okay, this is fascinating! *Transgress,* at least in this case, appears to mean *to miss the mark, (and so, not share in the prize).* (It also says it figuratively means *to err, especially to sin.*) So now I want to see the Greek translation for *heed*. It says (figuratively) *to hold the mind towards,* i.e., *pay attention to, be cautious about, apply oneself* to, *adhere to.*

So I'm understanding from these verses and translations that Christ is telling me to be cautious when someone misses the mark (or sins) against me. First, I need to *admonish* them. (One Greek translation says admonish means *to caution* or *gently reprove.*) In other words, I need to let them know that something's not okay by cautioning them or gently reproving them. (The word reprove reminds me of a verse in D&C 121 that I love. It says the Spirit sometimes moves upon you to reprove with sharpness, but then you have to show forth greater love afterwards so you aren't esteemed as an enemy. I've studied *sharpness* before, and I was happy to learn that it can mean *to clarify* rather than to speak harshly.)

Okay, back to Luke 17:3. It says if the offender repents, I have to forgive him. So how does God expect me to determine if he's repented? Or does he really expect me to? I wonder if there is a JST about that. No. But there is a footnote linking this verse to Matthew 18:15. I quickly look that up. It says, "Moreover if thy brother shall trespass against thee, go and tell him his fault between thee and him alone: if he shall hear thee, thou hast gained thy brother."

Now there is an awesome reason to do my best to resolve trespasses! I gain a brother or sister instead of an enemy! Wouldn't it be awesome if we could all learn to communicate our feelings when someone misses the mark and offends us? Christ's hope for us is that we would forgive one another and gain a brother. He's always encouraging us to free ourselves of our natural man garbage so we can live joyfully!

Going back to my question about that "if he repent" clause, it looks like it might be answered in verse 4. It says I forgive him every time he says he repents, even if it happens a zillion times in the same day! Okay, My Beloved Savior, what are you trying to tell me? I think you may very likely be trying to help me to never take offense! After all, that would be the most freeing, joyful way to live! That's how I want to be. Please soften my heart and help me to live free of judgment. Help me have the wisdom and courage to handle things this way when something distresses me.

Okay, so my study time is long spent, but I happened to notice the verse that follows the command to forgive seven times seventy. "And the apostles said unto the Lord, Increase our faith." I don't know if those two verses are meant to be tied together, but to me it would make a ton of sense.

I have no idea why the apostles might have said that. But for myself, I say, "Oh, Dear Savior, I know of myself I could never forgive so freely. I want to, but I am so mortal! If I have any hope of forgiving as You entreat me to—and as You so generously forgave those who trespassed against You—I must have an increase of faith. Lord, I know the kind of faith I need can only come from Your wondrous grace. I know I have to love my brother and be free of judgment and criticism or I won't be willing to forgive over and over. It's not an easy thing You ask.

Still, I've experienced the pain that comes with a lack of forgiveness, and that's not easy either. I've seen it destroy people I dearly love. We need repentance in our lives. It frees us! Thank You for teaching us this beautiful principle, and for showing us the way to live it. Please increase my faith so that I can freely walk in the light of Your perfect love. I desire to walk the path of love, trespassing against no one, but sometimes things happen contrary to my desire. Thank You for helping me turn again to You, for helping me better understand repentance and forgiveness. You are my guiding light."

The "Wendy Watson Method" of searching the scriptures for answers

I highly recommend *Rock Solid Relationships* by Wendy Watson Nelson.[7] (Since first publishing this book, she married and has added her married name on more recent publications. For the sake of brevity, I have continued to use my original title for the scripture study method described in her book.) Here I share only a quick summary of the steps, and one personal example of a time when this method proved to be a lifesaver for me. Such has been the case on a number of occasions.

Steps of the Wendy Watson Method:

1. Explain the problem to God and ask Him the *one* question you most need answered that day.

2. Plead for the Holy Ghost to sit beside you and guide you as you read the word of the Lord.

3. Open the scriptures to whatever random page "and read until you find the answer."[8]

She said to read back and forth a bit, pondering and asking questions, until the Spirit directs you to your answer.

When I first read the third step it sounded bold to expect God to respond "on command," but I've been amazed and humbled each time I've sincerely applied this method. Softening my heart so that I'm ready and willing to seek an answer from the scriptures often takes longer than finding my answer!

Using the Wendy Watson Method to resolve a conflict with my daughter-in-law

I went to stay with our son's family after the birth of a new grandson. While my daughter-in-law was still in the hospital with the baby, I took care of the other four children. Within moments of my arrival, I noticed that our adorable two-year-old granddaughter was creating chaos in the home. I quickly implemented a gentle but decisive response that seemed to correct her disruptive behavior.

When my daughter-in-law came home from the hospital, I explained to her the consequence I was imposing. She agreed that it was a great way to deal with the problem.

However, the next evening I noticed a dramatic increase in my granddaughter's disruptive behavior. I also noticed that my daughter-in-law was not employing the consequences we had discussed. They were so simple and had relieved so much stress. It was frustrating to be back where we had started.

Assuming I just needed to review the plan and explain it more clearly, I approached my daughter-in-law. *Assuming* was my first mistake, approaching an exhausted mother who was dealing with postpartum hormones was my second mistake, and there were more to follow.

Early in the conversation I could tell we were headed for disaster. I immediately dropped the subject, but I had already shaken our relationship. It was obvious that I needed to let go of my wish to fix the problem, but I couldn't make myself stop thinking about this little girl's behavior.

The purpose of my visit was to be helpful, and correcting this problem seemed like the most helpful thing I could possibly do. Adjusting to the extra demands of a new baby in the home would be much easier without the two-year-old constantly creating havoc.

And we had been so close! All my daughter-in-law needed to do was consistently impose the consequences a little longer. It was beyond frustrating to watch all the progress fade away. Wasn't there something I could do?

That night it was almost one o'clock before I finally got the new baby to sleep. As I was getting ready for bed, my tired little brain continued to hash over the situation. My heart ached as I considered the harm I had done to our relationship in my effort to be helpful, but I still wanted to find a way to manage that two-year-old. In the midst of this turmoil, I wearily knelt to say my prayer.

As my knees touched the floor I glanced over and noticed my scriptures lying on the table. Immediately Sister Watson's method of seeking answers came to mind. "But it's so late," I protested. "Surely, Father, You don't want me to be up even later. I need to sleep *now* because the baby will wake up again in a few hours."

I tried to pray, but again the thought came that I should seek an answer from the scriptures. I argued with the Spirit as I tried to press on with my prayer, but finally I realized I was never going to win.

Reluctantly I flipped the pages open only to find my bleary eyes staring at the first chapter of Helaman. The name of the assassin, Kishkumen, was high-lighted on the page. "Great!" I thought. "How can there possibly be an answer to my problem in the story of a murder?" Though Sister Watson's method had always been effective on the first try before, I seriously considered closing my scriptures and opening them again in a different place.

As I debated, I began scanning the chapter. The first ten verses told of the death of the chief judge, Pahoran, and of the election that was held to select his replacement. Three of his sons (Pahoran, Pacumeni, and Paanchi) contended for the position.

When the voice of the people chose Pahoran, Pacumeni accepted the election results and united with his brother. However, Paanchi and his followers were angry and rebellious. They hired Kishkumen, who boldly killed the new chief judge as he sat on his judgment seat.

"Terrific," I thought. "Here I am at one o'clock in the morning reading about dastardly political intrigue when what I really need is a few good hours of sleep."

Then I realized that the word "unite" was stuck in my mind. Was the Spirit already trying to show me something? I reviewed the verses again, allowing my mind to quietly reflect on the story and seek the message it had to offer. As the Spirit began to point out the parallels between this story and my own situation, I wept.

God had chosen my daughter-in-law to be the mother-leader of this little child just as the voice of the people had chosen Pahoran to be their leader. The intended purpose of my visit was to be as Pacumeni and support my daughter-in-law. Instead, my heart had been as Paanchi's, thinking my way was better because it made so much sense to me.

The truth was clear and simple, and yet I had been blinded by my good intentions, too invested in my own ideas to see what I was actually doing. I'd been determined that my way was the right way, so I'd spent my energy looking for a way to manipulate my daughter-in-law into agreeing with me instead of asking for the Spirit's guidance. With this new perspective, the war in my heart easily ended.

An overwhelming sense of gratitude filled my soul as I considered the gentle way in which the Lord had reminded me of something I had already known. Of course I knew it was not my role to be in charge here. Putting my own will aside and uniting with my daughter-in-law was the Lord's solution to *my* problem. It was the best possible way for me to serve her.

As I crawled into bed at that late hour, I savored the sweet sense of love and gratitude that filled my heart—love for God, for His words, for my daughter-in-law, for my son, for their children, for my entire family, for all the goodness in my life. I expressed my gratitude for the words from the Book of Mormon—surprisingly from "the war chapters"—that had been my speedy vehicle to peace.

I cherish the relationship I have with each of my daughters-in-law, and that night I felt especially grateful to the Lord for showing me my faulty thinking before I created a situation that might require years to heal.

Although I did get up with the baby a few hours later, the next morning I arose unexpectedly refreshed. During the remaining days of my visit, I was able to serve my daughter-in-law in many different ways, happily strengthening our relationship. I was also able to observe my granddaughter's challenging behavior from a place of love, rather than being frustrated by my Molly Mormon desire to be in control and fix everything.

Example of capturing: Come Unto Me – March 2001

> Come unto me, all *ye* that labour and are heavy laden, and
> I will give you rest. Take my yoke upon you, and learn of
> me; for I am meek and lowly in heart: and ye shall find
> rest unto your souls. For my yoke *is* easy, and my burden is
> light. (Matthew 11:28–30)

My dear daughter Elona,

Come to me, your Savior, who stands with open arms, ready to
wrap you in a warm embrace if you will only take the few steps
to draw near to me. I see how you race around trying to make
everything right for everyone, trying to please everyone, trying
to impress everyone. You do many good things, many labors
which are good, but you often feel stressed because you believe
you aren't doing enough. I would gladly take your burden with
which you are heavy laden if you would draw near and give
it to me. You must learn of me. I can teach you if you will
trade your yoke of bondage for my yoke. Yes, you must always
wear a yoke, but my yoke is easy. The burden you pull is light
when my yoke is upon you. If you will only take my yoke, and
gratefully wear it always, you will find rest for your harried
soul. Rest—that joyous freedom from turmoil and doubt and
fear! That feeling of my total acceptance of you, just as you
are—that feeling you have thrilled to know before, however
fleetingly. This is what I want to give to you constantly.

What does the Savior mean when he says he is meek and lowly
in heart in this passage? Does he mean we can learn from him
because he is meek and lowly in heart, or is he pointing out
to us that we must be meek and lowly if we want to learn of
him? Is that an essential step for accepting his yoke? Would this
scripture be just as valid without that phrase?

Example of capturing: Learn of Me

> Learn of me, and listen to my words; walk in the meekness of my Spirit, and you shall have peace in me. (D&C 19:23)

Learn of me, your loving Savior, Elona, and listen to my words—I mean really listen. Don't go crazy trying to study them too deeply for now. Just savor them and believe what I say, just as a little child believes a loving parent. Walk in the meekness of my spirit, the gentle mercy I freely offer when you seek me with a humble heart, and you shall have peace in me. Peace, Elona! Remember? You know the unparalleled sweetness of my peace!

Bible customs and culture books

I've particularly enjoyed studying books by Kenneth E. Bailey to help me better understand Bible customs and culture. *Jesus Through Middle Eastern Eyes* and *The Cross and the Prodigal* are two of my favorites.[9] Donna Nielson's book, *Beloved Bridegroom*,[10] has deepened my understanding of the Savior's love by explaining ancient customs and culture. Lydia Mountford's *Jesus Christ in His Homeland* and *The King of the Shepherds and His Psalm* have also given me beautiful insights into Christ's tender care.[11] I'm eternally grateful to each of these authors. Because of their efforts I have a greater understanding of the breadth and depth of Christ's amazing love.

3. Cold Floors and Aching Knees

Meditation

Our electronic world keeps our lives and our minds so filled with noise that we may be uncomfortable with the quietness that invites the Spirit into our hearts. In a 1967 general conference address, President McKay emphasized the importance of introspective meditation which brings us to commune with God. This quote has inspired me and given me much food for thought over the years.

> We pay too little attention to the value of meditation, a principle of devotion. In our worship there are two elements: one is spiritual communion rising from our own meditation; the other, instruction from others, particularly from those who have authority to guide and instruct us. Of the two, the more profitable introspectively is meditation. Meditation is the language of the soul. It is defined as "a form of private devotion, or spiritual exercise, consisting in deep, continued reflection on some religious theme." Meditation is a form of prayer. We can say prayers without having any spiritual response. Meditation is one of the most secret, most sacred doors through which we pass into the presence of the Lord.[12]

Experiencing the Depths of Jesus Christ by Jeanne Guyon is a remarkable little book. (The intimate and endearing tone of the book may be partly explained by the fact that it was written in France in about 1685.) Its invitation to come to Christ through quiet, introspective contemplation is gently compelling. It is both simple and profound, both refreshing and joyful.

Guyon's methods of praying may seem unfamiliar in some ways, but I love pondering her ideas in relation to the scriptures she references. I've found interesting similarities in what she teaches and in what LDS scriptures teach. I've been fascinated by some of the parallels with my own experiences. I think anyone seeking to increase their ability to commune with God would benefit from reading this book.

I found a quote in the commentary at the end of the book which rang especially true to me. It speaks of the great chasm that must be bridged—regardless of the time in which we live—if we want to *know* God rather than just *know about* God.

> This is an age of endless reams of books and papers on endless varieties of subjects, an age that produces men who deliver mind-boggling lectures on the doctrine of prayer and yet know little of its deeper experience.[13]

I want to experience the deeper experience of Christ consistently throughout my life.

An immediate answer to a prayer for guidance

Just before my fifty-ninth birthday I sat contemplating some of the changes I had noticed in my abilities. My energy level no longer sustained a full day of rigorous activity, facts and phone numbers that I used to easily recall didn't come to mind when I needed them, and sometimes I completely forgot about appointments or other commitments. Although I was fully enjoying the grand-mothering stage of life, it occurred to me that I should ask God what He would like me to accomplish in the next several years while I still had significant physical and mental abilities available. I envisioned myself volunteering at a community center, or serving at the Missionary Training Center, or traveling to Central America to help with one of the many orphanages there.

Contemplating such possibilities generated an enthusiasm for a new adventure in my life, and after a while I knelt and began discussing my thoughts with God in a more formal way. Almost immediately these words popped into my mind: "Write your book."

I was stunned—but not stunned enough to prevent my mind from going into instant resistance mode. "But Father, You know I'm not a writer. It took me forever to get that article ready to publish a few years ago. Trying to respond to all of the suggestions of the editors nearly made me crazy, and I swore I would never do anything like that again!"

The Spirit offered no argument or further explanation, just a clear repetition of the previous words: "Write your book."

It took me a few weeks of reminding myself how grateful I am to be able to receive and recognize answers to prayer before I decided it was time to begin putting pen to paper.

At first it actually seemed like the project was going to flow pretty smoothly. I had a rough draft well under way within a few months. However, I soon discovered that honoring my guidance was not going to be as easy as I had hoped. Receiving such a definite answer—and having it reaffirmed from time to time—has kept me going in spite of lengthy interruptions and intermittent bouts of self-doubt.

4. You Can Watch *Johnny Lingo* Only So Many Times

The sacred sacrament covenant

President McKay said, "No more sacred ordinance is administered in the Church of Christ than the administration of the sacrament."[14]

When I first read that statement it surprised me. I'd always thought of the temple endowment as a more sacred ordinance than baptism or the sacrament since it's performed within the walls of the temple.

However, after more careful study, I stood corrected. I learned that when we partake of the sacrament each week, we are symbolically placing our hearts on God's altar—the sacrament table—and renewing *all* of our covenants. The frequent partaking of the sacrament helps us remember to keep ourselves unspotted from the world by renewing not only our baptismal covenants, but also our endowment, and marriage covenants. Perhaps that explains President McKay's statement.

For a long time I felt sorry for people who couldn't renew their temple covenants because they lived too far from a temple. Now I realize that, as far as renewing our covenants, we are all in the same boat. We *renew* our temple covenants when we partake of the sacrament. When we do temple work for the dead, we really only *review* our covenants. The blessing of renewal is available each week to almost all members. Thus, the sacrament is another lovely manifestation of God's love.

Trying to run away from Sabbath stress

When I arrived at the LTM (now MTC) to begin my mission, someone had posted a quote on the bedroom door that said,

"The best bridge between despair and hope is a good night's sleep." (It would be decades before I learned to fully embrace that possibility.) The following story is an example of how my Molly Mormon fears combined with emotional and physical exhaustion to create yet another miserable Sunday experience.

One Sunday I came home from church feeling especially angry and defeated. I quickly fixed lunch, got the baby down for her nap, and then told my husband I was leaving. When I saw the anxious look that sprang into his eyes, I felt a twinge of remorse. I sensed he was worried that I might be implying I didn't plan to return, but I was too worked up to respond to the compassion that tugged at my heart. My head felt like it was going to explode. All I could think of was running to a faraway place where no pain existed—where no sense of failure or lack of control could ever find me again. Fighting my tears, I silently turned and walked out the door.

As I backed out of the driveway my feelings of desperation increased. Where was I going? Everything in the world that really mattered to me was right there in that house—and yet they were making me crazy! What was I going to do? Who could I turn to?

I had some good friends, but I wasn't willing to approach anyone while I was in this frame of mind. My image would be ruined. Though it was acceptable—sometimes even entertaining— to hear women express their mothering frustrations in Relief Society lessons, it would be too humiliating to admit that I was actually running away from my family. The recurring thought that we were never going be good enough to get to the celestial kingdom consumed me. Why, oh why couldn't I be that wonderful Molly Mormon who knew how to make everything work out right?

After driving around for a long time, I parked at a church several miles from my home. I tried to read my scriptures, but I was too agitated to focus. Then I tried making a list of all the things I needed to do to get better control of my life. I didn't get far on that either. Finally I closed my eyes and fell asleep.

When I awakened a few hours later, the crisis was over. My stomach grumbled hungrily, but my real hunger was for my family. The nap had carried me across the bridge from despair to hope. With this much love in my heart, I was sure there *had* to be a way for us to make it to the celestial kingdom, and I was determined to find it! Bolstered by my newly found optimism, I hurried home to my loved ones.

Looking back, I know that if I had asked Monte to take care of the kids so I could sleep for a while, he would have been fine with it. But my pride wouldn't let me ask for help. I thought if he really cared, he would notice my need and *offer* his help. Besides, I didn't like how he "watched" the kids. Most often he just did his own thing, usually read a book; and he let the kids do their own thing, usually make a big mess for me to clean up. I thought he should maintain more control when I was gone. (Some great tools for handling that kind of mentality are shared in the Boundaries section of the appendix to chapter 7.)

A young woman's letter about being late for church

For years Robert and I couldn't be on time for church no matter what I did. I'd get everyone up early, I'd set our clothing out the night before, I'd get the kids in the car in plenty of time to arrive early, but nothing helped. We were always late. One morning I was so excited because we were in the car all set to arrive a few minutes early only to have

Robert insist that he needed to go back and check the oil in the car! We were late again.

I can't tell you how many Sundays we drove to church with me seething in the front seat. I was always angry with Robert for not being more committed to arriving on time, or angry with myself for not setting my alarm clock or not finding the kids' shoes ahead of time, or angry at the stake president for telling us we should actually be there TEN minutes early so we could quietly prepare ourselves for the meeting. Never mind that the stake president never arrived on time!

Finally, one Sunday as we got in the car, late again, the thought struck me that God was more interested in me loving my family and being happy and kind to them than having me arrive on time for church. He didn't want me to be angry with my family and set an unhappy tone for church. It was a wonderful aha moment.

Since then we have had many pleasant rides to church, and we are more able to enjoy the meeting once we get there, whether we arrive on time or not. I still try to get to church on time, but I believe the weightier matter is love—love for my family, and love for God.[15]

After I told Monte about this letter, he decided to check the sacrament meeting guidelines in the Church Handbook. They say:

The bishopric and the speakers should be in their seats at least five minutes before the meeting begins. ... The bishopric encourages families to *arrive on time* and to sit together.[16]

I've observed much distress and guilt over this issue through the years. There is the ideal, and then there is reality. When I had young children, my reality was much different than it is today. Now it's usually quite easy for me to arrive early. I can sing the whole sacrament hymn without interruption and actually focus on its message. I can focus on the prayers and the covenants I'm renewing. But not everyone in the congregation is in my situation. I hear babies and restless children. I sometimes see distraught parents. I'm glad they are all in attendance. Our common goal is to worship God together.

The bottom line, I believe, is to listen for the whisperings of the Spirit rather than feeling resentment toward leaders who are trying to be helpful, or maybe just trying to do their duty. They may have forgotten what it's like to deal with small children at church. They may have no clue what it's like to deal with a husband who's habitually late. I know that I'm happiest when I'm willing to cut everyone a whole lot of slack.

The Power of Keeping the Sabbath Day Holy

Whenever I think about the importance of honoring the Sabbath, my mind returns to Brother Groberg's October 1984 conference address.[17] It deeply stirred my heart the first time I heard it, and those feelings are powerfully renewed each time I review it. I highly recommend locating it on lds.org and thoughtfully pondering its message.

5. Let the Hunger Pains Begin

Fasting: A few thoughts and examples

Over the course of about a year, I fasted frequently for one of our sons because he was unemployed. Toward the end of that year, a visitor bore his testimony in our fast and testimony meeting and happened to mention something about his place of employment. The moment he named the company, the Spirit whispered that I needed to encourage my son to apply there.

Because of a couple of previous conversations, I knew my relationship with my son was somewhat strained at the time and I was concerned about how I might be received. However, the Spirit persisted so I decided I should take the risk.

Fortunately, my son welcomed my suggestion, and after several weeks of interviewing with the company he was hired. The job proved to be challenging in a variety of ways, and provided him with opportunities to develop his business abilities and his leadership skills. Though it didn't happen immediately, God answered me when I called, just as Isaiah said He would.[18]

I also fasted regularly for another son as he struggled to find employment soon after he got married. He and his new bride had moved to a university town where jobs were scarce and pay was low. His wife was able to get a minimum wage job within a few weeks, but our son continued to apply wherever he could without any success. He was deeply embarrassed to be living on his wife's income.

After several months he was finally offered a job at a space lab associated with the university. The pay was well above minimum wage, and the work dovetailed perfectly with his engineering classes. When he graduated, he accepted a full time position there. Now he's been happily employed by that same lab for about ten years.

Sometimes fasting precedes a change in circumstances as it did in these two examples, but other times it may precede a change in our hearts so that we can handle difficult circumstances. I'll share an example from my cousin's life.

Debbie was about six years older than I was. Her family lived in Salt Lake City, so we didn't see each other often. When she was a few months old a devastating illness left her body totally paralyzed. Her mind was clear and bright, but as she grew, her speech was only understandable to those who patiently listened to her distorted, broken words. It was an art I didn't develop until I was in my late teens.

Debbie's father worked for the welfare department of the Church in close association with Harold B. Lee, who was then an apostle. Everyone in the family was delighted when President Lee agreed to give her a blessing. She had received many blessings before, but never from an apostle.

In preparation for the blessing, family, friends, and ward members joined in a fast. All had great hopes that Debbie would finally be able to walk and talk, or at least experience a marked improvement in her health. No one was more deserving. She had borne her burdens well and had been faithful to the Lord in every way.

However, in the blessing President Lee didn't promise Debbie the restoration of her health. When he was through, he gently told the family that Debbie's faith and the faith of her family and friends was sufficient for her to be healed, but it was not the Lord's will. He said that her foreordained mission here on earth could not be fulfilled if she were healed.

No one wanted Debbie to spend the rest of her life trapped in her paralyzed body, but there was great comfort in the knowledge that their faith was acceptable to God and that her condition had a purpose. This knowledge strengthened the family as they continued to love and serve Debbie in her difficult condition.

Debbie lived into her mid-thirties, blessing countless lives with her faith, her positive attitude, and her sense of humor. She received her endowment sitting in a wheel chair. Deceased ancestors appeared to her on that occasion. From time to time her pains were eased as she entertained angels.

I'm grateful I had the opportunity to hear and understand Debbie's broken words. I'm also grateful I had the opportunity to fast for her, even though she never had the opportunity to walk. I'm grateful she shared her sacred experiences with us.

Regardless of how our fasting and prayers are rewarded, I know God loves His children, and that all things will work together for our good as we seek to know and do His will.

The joy of fasting with new understanding

Journal entry 2005: Fasting for our son Michael has brought me peace and joy that I haven't known in a fast before. That's because I now know how to fast, pray, and exercise my faith so much better than I used to! I know the Lord loves each of His children infinitely, and I believe that He allows us to experience things that will help us fulfill our divine potential. I trust that Michael is in God's loving hands. It helps me dismiss much of the worry that would have plagued me in earlier times.

What a blessing it is to have a greater understanding of gospel principles!

It also brings me great joy to know that our other children are fasting and praying for Michael. My heart is filled when I see our children supporting each other, and hear them express their love and concern for one another. This experience has renewed my personal testimony that there is real power in the faith, fasting, and prayers of loved ones. We have all benefited from Michael's struggle.

Fasting for the choir

Journal entry 2011: Being choir director is a challenging calling for me. We have wonderful choir members, but choir isn't anyone's first priority, so practices are often poorly attended. When we are scheduled to sing, we aren't always as prepared as we would like to be, and that was particularly the case today. I emailed everyone earlier in the week and asked them to come before sacrament meeting so we could go through the number, but I was still feeling very nervous about it.

Last night I decided to fast. In my prayer this morning I talked with God about the goodness of our choir members and how much I appreciate working with them to build His kingdom. I repeated mantras (words of faith) several times to dismiss fears that kept popping into my head.

Many choir members came for the rehearsal, and we worked through a lot of little finishing details that we hadn't focused on before. In the end, we gave a lovely performance in spite of our meager preparations. I felt joyfully calm and inspired as we sang The Lord's Prayer. Thank You, Father!

6. Even My Hosanna Shout Was a Flop

The body is a temple

Becoming familiar with temple ordinances and language allows me to take the temple with me wherever I go. The scriptures teach that our bodies are holy. Christ spoke of His body being a temple,[19] and Paul reminds us that we are the holy temple of God and that the Spirit of God (the Holy Ghost) dwells in us.[20] If I am truly a temple of God, then at anytime, anywhere, I can go within this temple body and experience God at the deepest level. (See Appendix entry for chapter 4 about *Experiencing the Depth of Jesus Christ*.)

Temples are meant to be a place where God reveals himself to His children. Respecting and honoring my "body temple" helps me receive revelation as I ponder the things of His kingdom— whether I am within the four walls of a temple, in a beautiful mountain setting, in a quite spot in our home, in a sacrament meeting, peacefully driving my car, or even in the shower.

Mental quietness, wherever I can achieve it, provides fertile ground for revelation. God desires to reveal Himself to His children. Temples symbolize that desire. Our challenge is to prepare ourselves to receive His revelation at any moment and in every circumstance.

A helpful book about the temple

Endowed from on High: Understanding the Symbols of the Endowment by John D. Charles.[21] His gift for clearly paralleling the scriptures and temple symbolism has blessed and strengthened my understanding of the endowment.

Thoughts about agency and forever families

Because of current circumstances, it appears very unlikely that I'll ever be in the temple with all of my children in this life, and perhaps not the next. Again, I find peace in leaving that in God's hands. Though as parents we make covenants in the temple that give us eternal family ties, agency is an irrevocable, individual gift. As it says in the hymn, "Know This, That Every Soul Is Free," I'm certain that "God will *force* no man to heaven."[22]

Likewise, it is clearly an ungodly desire for me to think I should somehow force my unwilling child—who is actually my spiritual peer—into the celestial kingdom. According to a revelation Joseph Smith received, I will inherit the glory I'm most comfortable with, and so will each of my children.[23] Though some people have felt inclined to scold me because they think I've given up on my child, nothing could be further from the truth. My love for God and my trust in His wisdom have simply superseded my fears and my personal desires.

"Your sons have a Savior"

I was at a fireside one evening when a man named Scott shared a profound experience. He said he had been shocked and horrified when he learned that his two young sons, 11 and 14, were experimenting with drugs and alcohol. Over the next couple of years, he and his wife sought the Spirit and did everything they could to "fix" their boys. They tried various restrictions, drug tests, a lie detector, and counseling, but nothing seemed to help.

In the midst of all this trouble, Scott went to the Salt Lake Temple, where he saw a picture of Christ calming the sea. As he sensed the panic of the scene, his eyes fastened on one of the disciples who was gritting his teeth and straining on a rope attached to the sail. The following words are taken from Scott's blog.

> As I stood in the temple that morning, the eyes of my understanding were opened and I suddenly saw myself in this painting. I was grasping on to the rope (my sons) as tightly as I could. I somehow felt that if I was strong enough, or good enough, or held on tight enough, I could save my two sons, just as this disciple thought he could save the boat. The Savior on the other hand didn't need to use any physical strength at all; without holding tightly to anything, He spoke the words, "Peace, be still," and the elements obeyed.[24]

After he pondered those thoughts, the Spirit whispered, "Scott, let go of the rope and trust Me. Your sons have a Savior, and it's not you!"

The Lord has offered me this same reminder over and over again. The Savior fulfills His role perfectly. He does His work on His own timetable and in His own wisdom. I can spend my life being distraught with how things are, or I can follow Christ's example by doing my best to fulfill my own work of love.

Experience at the Nauvoo Temple

When Monte and I visited Nauvoo in 2009, the whole trip was amazing, but I especially cherish one particular experience. Our tour group had been bussed to the temple so that we could attend a session. Monte and I ended up standing in line on the street while the temple recommends of others were being checked. We moved slowly toward the door, chatting with friends about the sites we had enjoyed visiting earlier in the day.

However, the moment I set my foot on the first step of the temple, a sudden feeling of holiness swept over me and all my previous thoughts were quickly forgotten. Then words flowed into my mind, telling me that I was on sacred ground, and that the work restored in this temple was not of this world.

The intensity of the feeling didn't last long, but each time I reflect on that experience, it enlivens my heart and invites me to offer my own private Hosanna Shout.

My temple experiences can still be rather routine

Lest anyone mistakenly think that I now jump to a high spiritual plane every time I enter the temple, I relate this experience. One Saturday morning I was working on my temple chapter and decided I would seek some guidance by going to the temple. (It seemed like an obvious thing to do!)

As I was putting my clothing bag in the car, I realized that I hadn't yet eaten breakfast. I didn't want my stomach to be growling during the session, so I delayed long enough to eat a piece of toast and a big bowl of cereal. On my way out the door, I grabbed several plums which I ate as I drove to Provo.

The timing was such that I didn't wait in the chapel more than a couple of minutes before entering the endowment room. As I took my seat, I reviewed some of the things I had previously written. I silently prayed that the Spirit would call to my mind pertinent ideas that I should include, or that I would at least receive some kind of guidance in regards to my writing.

That session did indeed provide me with a significant lesson about temple attendance. I learned that you shouldn't eat too much before you go to a session, or you will spend a lot of time struggling to stay awake!

A sweet thought that came to me in the temple

After completing an uneventful session, I lingered in the celestial room as I usually do. Sitting in a chair facing a huge picture of Christ, I let go of my hope for some striking insight and just relaxed into the peacefulness of the moment. After a few minutes, I closed my eyes and offered a silent prayer of gratitude. When I opened my eyes, I noticed that the room was beginning to fill with Hispanic brothers and sisters. Apparently a Spanish session had followed the session I attended.

Even though I didn't recognize anyone in the room, my heart swelled with love for these wonderful people as I watched them embrace each other and quietly rejoice in the sweetness of being there together. Then a powerful thought came to my mind. Though in one way I was an outsider since I didn't know any of them, in God's eternal family, there are no outsiders.

Thoughts stimulated by a young wife's statement

As I worked on this chapter, I asked a few people how they feel about the temple. One young mother responded, "I've learned that going to the temple with your spouse regularly doesn't mean that you will have a happy marriage."

Realizing that my temple marriage didn't mean eternal bliss was a harsh reality for me as well. I learned that patience, compassion, and respect are relationship skills that must be developed and practiced in daily life, moment by moment, outside of the temple. Once we were married, they didn't come as automatically as they had when we were dating.

However, I've found that when I leave the temple after feeling the Lord's divine love, I'm blessed with the desire and the humility to practice godly qualities. As I have prayerfully sought the Lord's guidance both in and out of the temple, I have been guided to people and books that have helped me understand how to go about improving my relationship skills.

A funny thing happened on the way to the temple!

On one occasion many years ago, my early morning temple attendance brought an encounter with a police officer. He had stealthily trailed me as I disregarded several red traffic lights before pulling into the temple parking lot. I explained to him that I had deliberately run all those lights—after slowing almost to a stop and checking for cross traffic—because I was nervous about sitting alone on the dark streets of Provo when there were no other vehicles in sight. My explanation left him bemused and speechless. Finally he said he wasn't quite sure if what I had done was a good idea or not. Then he wished me an enjoyable time in the temple and drove away.

I can't say that I enjoyed my temple experience that day any more than I had any other, but I did profusely thank the Lord that I hadn't been given a ticket. The best part of my day was the look on my husband's face when I got home and told him about the befuddled police officer.

7. Neighbors—Who Needs Them?

Boundaries

For anyone who wants to understand the importance of boundaries and the healing influence they can have on troubled relationships, I heartily recommend a book called, *Boundaries: When to Say Yes, How to Say No to Take Control of Your Life.*[25]

The value of the ideas in this book was reinforced to me because of an experience I had with a young woman named Jessica.

Jessica had been one of the happiest and most pleasant young people I had ever known. However, several years after her temple marriage, she came to me with a broken heart, confiding that she had to talk to someone—even if it meant violating the rule that you shouldn't talk to others about your marriage problems.

After assuring her that this "rule" had been greatly distorted to the detriment of many marriages, she began to pour out the painful details of her relationship. She told me that from the very beginning of their marriage, her husband had criticized her incessantly. Anytime he was around, she walked on eggshells, wondering what might send him off on his next tirade.

She felt like she could never do anything right, and that he was impossible to please. Each morning she tried to wait to start her housework until he was gone. She didn't want to listen to his comments about how she was doing everything wrong, or hear his demeaning tone of voice telling her how she "should" be doing things.

She resented his constant criticism, but she saw no hope for improvement. She had been taught that people can't change their spouses, they can only change themselves. Consequently she felt trapped, doomed to deal with her husband's negativity forever unless the Holy Ghost somehow inspired him to change.

Throughout their marriage she had earnestly prayed, attended the temple, studied the scriptures, pored over the marriage advice of general authorities, and read many books on relationships. As far as she knew, she had done everything she could to be a better marriage partner.

Later she learned that her husband had also been trying to figure out how to improve their marriage. He worked hard every day for the family, attended church and the temple, and prayed to know how to be a better husband.

Despite their efforts, whenever she tried to talk to him about her concerns, he would get frustrated and say she was just too sensitive. At times she experienced so much pain that she found it difficult to pray. All she could do was beg God—if He cared at all about her and her family—to intervene and save them.

After years of feeling criticized and disregarded, she finally came to a breaking point. She felt too emotionally beaten down— too exhausted and hopeless—to go on. She cared deeply for her husband and had no desire to hurt him. He was a good father to their children and had other wonderful character traits. However, she knew she must either find a way to change their relationship or to end the marriage. That is when she came to me.

I have long believed that most marriages are worth saving and that our culture tends to give up on marriage too easily. But as this young woman shared the details of their relationship and all the things she had done in her attempts to improve it, the best suggestion I could offer was a trial separation. Maybe if they were apart for a while, her husband would decide that he cared enough to work on the relationship, even if he still believed she was "too sensitive."

With Jessica's permission, I discussed her situation with Monte that evening. He reminded me of the *Boundaries* book we had read together sometime earlier, and we immediately gave her a copy.

Jessica quickly connected with the familiar scriptural approach which the authors used to substantiate the principles they taught.

A few days later, she and her children went on a trip to visit some friends and family members. Because of work commitments, her husband didn't travel with them so the trip provided some immediate relief from the stress in their marriage. While Jessica was away, she studied and prayed about things that needed to change for their marriage to survive.

The *Boundaries* book begins with a discussion about the necessity of fences. It explains that fences are physical boundaries which clearly define where a specific property begins and ends. The owner alone is responsible for what happens on his property. Fences have gates so that the owner can choose what he lets into his property and what goes out from it. When people have no fences, or they let their fences fall into disrepair, they often get angry or complain about trespassers. They don't realize that the problem may very well lie with the condition of their fences. They may even become trespassers on the property of others.

The book explains that "In the spiritual world, fences are invisible. Nevertheless, you can create good protective fences with your words. The most basic boundary setting word is *no*. It lets others know that you exist apart from them and that you are in control of you."[26]

Early on, the authors share an example of a woman who came to them, frustrated that her mature son was still depending on her to meet his needs. To help her see what was happening in their relationship, she was given the example of a man who set his sprinklers to water his neighbor's yard. Of course the neighbor was delighted with his green lawn, but he never learned how to set his own sprinklers and take care of his own yard.

As Jessica pored over the *Boundaries* book, she began to see the role she had played in creating much of the conflict in her marriage. She realized that rather than taking responsibility for her feelings and communicating them to her husband, she had blamed *him* for their conflicts and their circumstances. She also came to realize that she did not respect herself, and that she had no confidence in her right as an equal partner in the marriage. As a result, she had been timid about approaching her husband when challenging issues arose.

Whenever she *had* mustered the courage to bring up a problem, she'd felt totally disregarded and shut down. Her response had usually been to clam up and pretend that everything was fine. Her natural cheeriness was stifled and she'd become sullen, defensive, sarcastic, and argumentative. This frustrated her husband because he thought everything was fine, and that she ought to be happy. She recognized that it had been hard on him to be stuck with a miserable wife when he thought he was marrying a pleasant, engaging young woman.

The *Boundaries* book helped Jessica realize that she was afraid of confrontation because she didn't know how to address issues in a way that would bring her and her husband closer together. As she embraced the idea that it was okay for her to feel *whatever* she was feeling, she quickly regained her sense of self-respect. She finally understood that she was responsible for her own feelings and for making them known to her husband and others. She was greatly relieved to learn that she was *not* responsible for her husband's feelings or for his happiness.

Jessica was actually excited to see the part that she had played in their endless conflicts. At last she understood how she could create a positive change in the relationship. She began to pray for guidance to help her establish appropriate boundaries from a place of love.

In her new frame of mind, answers flowed steadily to her. She was sure her husband wouldn't like many of them, but she felt certain that setting boundaries was their only hope. After more prayer, she invited him to spend some time discussing their marriage and the things they each thought needed to change for them to be happy.

Jessica felt greatly empowered by the truths she was learning. In very clear language, this naturally non-confrontational young woman told her already hurt and confused husband that she would no longer accept being told that her feelings didn't matter, or that she was too sensitive. She also told him that she would no longer be monitored, criticized, or told what to do. She did her best to explain that she had no desire to attack him, but that she wanted him to be aware of the changes she was making in her life.

It was a pivotal moment in their marriage.

As a result of this first discussion, they decided to have a formal "meeting" every Sunday. During these talks they would discuss the previous week and the upcoming week. They would make plans together and ask how they could support each other. They agreed to write down things that bothered them during the week and not bring them up until their Sunday discussion time.

To set the tone they wanted, they decided to start their talks with a lot of positive things. They established a formal agenda to follow which started with each of them expressing appreciation for something the other had done the previous week. Then they each shared something from the previous week that they had especially enjoyed. Next, they talked about their family and individual needs for the upcoming week, and how they could support each other. Finally, they discussed any touchy subjects and did their best to resolve their conflicts.

It was not comfortable for either of them to be as open, honest, and patient as they needed to be—and there were some intense moments—but as they ventured into this new territory, miracles gradually began to happen. Within six months, they were beginning to feel like friends again.

Now, years later, Jessica and her husband continue to keep in touch with us. They are both very grateful that they went through the pain of this transition and stayed in the marriage. They still have their Sunday discussions, but they are more casual now. Both of them have become quite skilled at communicating and resolving issues in a respectful way whenever the need arises. Both feel heard and supported. They are so thankful for the positive changes that have happened in their marriage, and they attribute much of their success to understanding the concepts found in the *Boundaries* book.

One thing they have had to discuss a lot over the years is their differing opinions about how money should be managed. Establishing a budget based on principles found in Dave Ramsey's Financial Peace University materials[27] has helped them immensely.

Another thing that has made a huge difference for them is establishing priorities. Jessica's husband is self-employed and often wants her help with his business calls and projects. He used to make numerous requests and then become irritated if she didn't follow through with them very quickly. Meanwhile she felt overwhelmed and irritated because he seemed to expect her to do whatever he asked regardless of what else she needed to do in her day. And no matter what she *did* do, she rarely felt appreciated because he expected her to have done more.

During one of their discussions, Jessica expressed to her husband her deep desire to be supportive. However, she explained that she was not willing to immediately put her life of hold every time he asked her to do something. She then taped a piece of paper on the fridge and told him that he could have three active requests on the list at a time. She said she would do them as soon as she could work them in with the other demands in her life. After she crossed one off, he was free to put another one on.

This worked very well for both of them. It helped her husband feel supported, and it helped her feel respected. When the requests were written down and limited to three, she didn't easily forget then, and she didn't have to hear an agitated tone of voice when the requests were made.

Jessica is thrilled with the changes in her marriage, and so is her husband. They are both much happier now as individuals and as a couple. Since Jessica learned to set boundaries, her husband has also gained a new sense of freedom. He's learning to set boundaries with employees, with extended family members, and even with her.

The *Boundaries* book taught Jessica and her husband to speak a new language. It's a language of respect and cooperation. It's a language that builds genuine love. It's a language of peace, faith, and joy. It's based on the belief that marriage partners are a team, working together to create the lives they want by confronting issues in a way that strengthens the marriage.

Jessica and her husband praise God continually for giving them the tools to save their family. In my opinion, both Jessica and her husband deserve great accolades for the excellent work they have done (and continue to do) on their relationship.

Bailey on the first and second great commandments

I love what Kenneth Bailey says about the first and second great commandments in his wonderfully insightful book, *Jesus Through Middle Eastern Eyes*.

> Jesus placed "love God" before the commandment to "love your neighbor." The order is important. Experience dictates that it is very hard to love the unloving neighbor until the disciple's *heart is filled with the love of God*, which *provides the energy and motivation* necessary for the [sometimes] arduous task of loving the neighbor.[28]

He goes on to say that if we love others with the expectation of love coming back to us, we may give up in frustration and disappointment. But if we love out of gratitude for God's love, God's love sustains us.

Thoughts on commandments

Journal entry March 2011: Every commandment from God offers freedom, and freedom brings joy. The first great commandment to love God frees my heart from the fear of man and of the world in general. When my heart is free, it is flooded with love for God and with the guidance of the Spirit. The second great commandment frees me of competing with God's children, of fearing them, of wanting power or dominion over them. Love for others and more guidance from the Spirit can then enter. Out goes pride, out goes envy, out goes coveting—and everything else that makes me unhappy. All of the commandments related to my confessions fall under the umbrella of these two great commandments—

prayer, Sabbath day observance, fasting, temple attendance, and scripture study—help me in my efforts to love God, which then invites me to love my neighbor. It really is all about love! God is love!

Gratitude

Journal entry March 2011: Tonight I was again overwhelmed by the joy and freedom I felt as I picked up my scriptures and a flood of love poured over me. It brought to mind how guilty and worthless I used to feel when I noticed my scriptures sitting on my shelf before my heart was changed. I couldn't help weeping in gratitude. I was still feeling tender when Monte and I knelt for our prayer together, so when he asked about my tears I explained. "Every day I feel God's love. Every day I hold my scriptures in my hands, and even on days when I haven't taken the time to read or capture, I don't feel guilt. I feel love. I feel joy! I know such a different God than I experienced in my childhood, my youth, and my early mothering." This is why I glory in my Jesus. He is my strength, not my tormenter. He is my rock. His love anchors me. His grace frees me to learn. My love for Him makes all of this possible. I love Him because He first loved me, but then He always loved me. I just didn't know it.

NOTES

Introduction: Falling off the Molly Mormon Pedestal

1. Elona K. Shelley, "You Just Have to Love," http://segullah.org/
   spring2006/havelove.html. My revised copy is on my website at
   www.ElonaShelley.com.

1. God and His Tattletale Angels

1. "Do What Is Right," Hymns, no. 237. Text: Anon., The Psalms of Life,
   Boston, 1857.
2. "Dearest Children, God Is Near You," Hymns, no. 96. Text: Charles L.
   Walker, 1832–1904; in 1880 hymnbook.
3. Matthew 24:40–41.
4. Dallin H. Oaks, "Miracles," Ensign, June 2001.
5. Alma 5:26; emphasis added.

2. The Iron Rod as a Weapon of Self-Destruction

1. Colleen C. Harrison, He Did Deliver Me from Bondage (Hyrum, UT:
   Windhaven Publishing, 2002). Note: He Did Deliver Me from Bondage
   20th Anniversary Edition, 2012, is published by Hearthaven Publishing,
   Hyrum, UT (www.hearthavenpublishing.com).
2. Mosiah 29:20.
3. Alma 32:27.
4. Gordon B. Hinckley, "The Light within You," Ensign, May 1995.
5. LDS View™ is a Church scripture program. A Windows version can be
   downloaded at http://ldsview.byu.edu. You can then download the scriptures
   in 30 languages. LDS View is the Church version of WordCruncher˙ which
   was developed at Brigham Young University. WordCruncher for Windows is
   a free download at www.wordcruncher.com. A version for iPhones and iPads
   should be available in the last half of 2013. With WordCruncher, you can
   download Webster's 1844 dictionary, Shakespeare, and other ebooks. As

other religious ebooks are added, you will be notified. You will also be able to see the LDS View scriptures.

6 Wendy Watson Nelson, *Rock Solid Relationships: Strengthening Personal Relationships with Wisdom from the Scriptures*, (Salt Lake City, UT: Deseret Book, 2003).

7 Luke 15:20.

8 Kenneth E. Bailey, *The Cross and the Prodigal: Luke 15 Through the Eyes of Middle Eastern Peasants* (Downers Grove, IL: InterVarsity Press, 2005). For other books relating to Bible customs and culture, see the appendix.

9 Bailey, *The Cross and the Prodigal*, 67.

10 Spencer W. Kimball, "How Rare a Possession—the Scriptures," *Ensign*, September 1976.

3. Cold Floors and Aching Knees

1 "A Child's Prayer," *Children's Songbook*, 12; Words and music: Janice Kapp Perry © 1984 by Janice Kapp Perry; used by permission of author.

2 Alma 36:21.

4. You Can Watch *Johnny Lingo* Only So Many Times

1 Luke 14:5.

2 D&C 59:9–10; emphasis added.

3 Isaiah 58:13.

4 D&C 84:24.

5 The *Liken* movie series is produced by Lightstone Pictures, LLC. (Provo, UT), http://www.likenthescriptures.com.

6 Isaiah 59:13–14.

7 David O. McKay, *Teachings of Presidents of the Church: David O. McKay* (Salt Lake City: The Church of Jesus Christ of Latter-day Saints, 2011), 34.

5. Let the Hunger Pains Begin

1 D&C 50:13–14.

2 Isaiah 58:6.

3 New International Version (NIV). Several Bible translations can be found online at http://blueletterbible.org.

4 Isaiah 61:1–3.

6. Even My Hosanna Shout Wasn't Good Enough

[1] S. Michael Wilcox, "That All Their Outgoings from This House May Be in the Name of the Lord," http://ce.byu.edu/cw/womensconference/archive/2000/wilcox_michael.htm.

[2] Ezekiel 47.

[3] Ether 1:42. See also Exodus 29:42.

[4] See "The Body Is a Temple" in the supplemental information for this chapter in the Appendix.

7. Neighbors—Who Needs Them?

[1] Luke 2:14.

[2] Alma 39:9.

[3] The Arbinger Institute, *The Anatomy of Peace: Resolving the Heart of Conflict* (San Francisco: Berrett-Koehler Publishers, Inc., 2006). The Arbinger Institute and people associated with it have published several books that have helped me learn to love others as prompted by the Spirit. Some of these include: *Leadership and Self-Deception* (Arbinger Institute, 2000, http://www.arbinger.com); *Bonds that Make us Free: Healing Our Relationships, Coming to Ourselves* (C. Terry Warner, 2001); "Honest, Simple, Solid, True" (C. Terry Warner, BYU Devotional, 16 January 1996, http://speeches.byu.edu), *The Peacegiver: How Christ Offers to Heal our Hearts and Homes* (James L. Ferrell, 2004); and *The Holy Secret* (James L. Ferrell, 2008).

[4] Matthew 10:19.

[5] 1 Nephi 11:21–23; emphasis added.

[6] Moroni 7:46, 48.

Conclusion: I Glory in My Jesus!

[1] D&C 95:6.

[2] Isaiah 61:3.

[3] 2 Nephi 33:6.

[4] 2 Nephi 31:20.

[5] Matthew 20:9.

[6] D&C 90:24; 98:3; 100:15; 105:40; Romans 8:28.

[7] 2 Nephi 4:16–19.

[8] 2 Nephi 4:16–20; emphasis added.

⁹ Monte and I have been greatly influenced by the life and teachings of Chauncey C. Riddle. Some of his writings are available at www.sviewp.com and www.ChaunceyRiddle.com.

¹⁰ Matthew 5:48.

¹¹ Matthew 5:48 footnote, and Strong's Greek dictionary. Monte told me this word was also used to refer to a person who had *completed* the preparatory "temple ordinances" needed to stand before God (John W. Welch, *Illuminating the Sermon at the Temple & Sermon on the Mount,* [Provo, UT: Foundation for Ancient Research and Mormon Studies, 1999], chapter 4, http://mi.byu.edu). In the Book of Mormon, Jesus gave the "Sermon on the Mount" at the temple to temple-going people. Welch's book helps one see the parallels between the sermon and temple ordinances.

¹² Genesis 6:9 footnote and Strong's Hebrew dictionary. When my friend did similar research, her favorite translation of this Hebrew word was "whole-hearted." (Jewish Publication Society, *JPS Bible* [1917], Genesis 6:9; 17:1; Deuteronomy 18:13; Job 1:1; http://www.mechon-mamre.org).

¹³ John 6:66–67.

¹⁴ John 6:68–69; emphasis added.

¹⁵ Mosiah 4:26–27.

¹⁶ 1 Corinthians 2:9.

¹⁷ See Matthew 11:28; D&C 19:23; Isaiah 55:7.

¹⁸ 2 Nephi 2:25.

Appendix

¹ Proverbs 3:5–6.

² Bonnie D. Parkin, "Feel the Love of the Lord," *Ensign,* May 2002, 84; "Eternally Encircled in His Love," *Ensign,* November 2006.

³ Mosiah 26:30.

⁴ 3 Nephi 13:14–15; Matthew 6:14–15.

⁵ Wanda West Palmer, "Oh, That I Were an Angel" (Jackson Music Corp.).

⁶ Alma 29:1.

⁷ Nelson, *Rock Solid Relationships.*

⁸ Nelson, *Rock Solid Relationships,* 11.

⁹ Bailey, *The Cross and the Prodigal* and Kenneth E. Bailey, *Jesus Through Middle Eastern Eyes: Cultural Studies in the Gospels* (Downers Grove, IL: InterVarsity Press, 2008).

[10] Donna B. Nielsen, *Beloved Bridegroom* (Salt Lake City: Onyx Press, 1999).

[11] Lydia M. Von Finkelstein Mountford, *Jesus Christ in His Homeland* (Cincinnati, OH: Press of Jennings and Graham, 1911), and *The King of the Shepherds and His Psalm* (Cincinnati, OH: Abingdon Press, 1914).

[12] McKay, *Teachings of Presidents of the Church*, 31–32; "Consciousness of God: Supreme Goal of Life," *Improvement Era,* June 1967, 80–82.

[13] Jeanne Guyon, *Experiencing the Depths of Jesus Christ* (Jacksonville, FL: SeedSowers Publishing, 1975), 148. This book is also titled *A Method of Prayer* or *A Short Method of Prayer.*

[14] McKay, *Teachings of Presidents of the Church*, 34; Conference Report, April 1946, 111–116.

[15] Personal letter from the young mother.

[16] *Handbook 2: Administering the Church*, 18.2.2; emphasis added.

[17] John H. Groberg, "The Power of Keeping the Sabbath Day Holy," *Ensign,* November 1984.

[18] Isaiah 58:9.

[19] John 2:21.

[20] 1 Corinthians 3:16–17.

[21] John D. Charles, *Endowed from on High: Understanding the Symbols of the Endowment* (Springville, UT: Horizon Publishers, 2004, 2007, 2012).

[22] "Know This, That Every Soul Is Free," *Hymns,* no. 240. Text: Anon., ca. 1805, Boston. Included in the first LDS hymnbook, 1835.

[23] D&C 88:22–33.

[24] Scott Webb, Blog, January 14, 2012, http://thegospelaccordingtoscott.blogspot.com/2012_01_01_archive.html.

[25] Henry Cloud and John Townsend, *Boundaries: When to Say YES, When to Say NO, To Take Control of Your Life,* (Grand Rapids, MI: Zondervan Pub. House, 1992).

[26] Cloud, *Boundaries*, 34.

[27] Dave Ramsey, *Financial Peace University,* http://daveramsey.com.

[28] Bailey, *Jesus Through Middle Eastern Eyes*, 287; emphasis added.

ABOUT THE AUTHOR

Elona K. Shelley spent her childhood in Moore, Idaho, a small farming community in the heart of the Lost River Valley. After attending three years of college at the University of Idaho, she served a mission in Central America. She attended BYU where she met and married Monte Shelley. As an elementary school teacher she was responsible for a diverse group of fourth graders. She gave birth to her first child seven days after his due date and three days after school got out. Since then she has focused her life studies on mothering, grand-mothering, caring for aging parents, serving joyfully, and getting to know God better.

Elona is grateful for the callings she has had in Relief Society and Young Women. Those years of service have helped her become aware of many who experience similar feelings to her own. Besides the things discussed in *Confessions of a Molly Mormon*, Elona's spirit is also nurtured by the outdoors, good books, and sharing thoughts and feelings with anyone who wants to chat.

Today Elona and her husband, Monte, enjoy living in Orem, Utah where they welcome a steady stream of family and friends into their home.

You can find more of Elona's writing at www.ElonaShelley.com.